The Luck of the Draw

My Story

Battling Cancer and Thriving

Sandra Pickles

The following pages contain true stories regarding the author's cancer journey and treatments. In some cases, the specific details and names have been changed or omitted to protect their privacy.

For more information, email sandrapickles60@gmail.com

ISBN: 979-8-88759-874-1 - paperback

ISBN: 979-8-88759-875-8 - ebook

ISBN: 979-8-88759-876-5 - hardcover

This book is for ...

This book is for all those humble heroes who stand stoic and calm in the face of the storm and who draw on swords of courage when they need to be strong.

This story is for anyone and everyone who has lived life at its best and at what may seem its worst. It is for any person who has experienced not just cancer, but any disease or situation that leads them and those who love them to veer off the path in life they had previously chosen. I wish to give a long and loud shout-out to those friends and family members who follow those souls so sadly stricken down on that jagged path they are forced to follow, to catch them when they fall. No matter how much it hurts those who suffer from a disease, I believe at times it's those who stand witness to their pain and suffering and are helpless in healing it who hurt the most. This book is for my mother, Darlene May Fraser, and my brother-in-law Roger Burris, who also suffered from multiple myeloma.

This book is dedicated to my husband Dave, my hero, who stands firmly by my side through this journey and all others.

Table of Contents

"The Luck of The Draw"

"It's just the luck of the draw," was all they could say,
Was the cause for the cancer they said I might have on that day.

I sat there in shock as they said they could see,
A concern that something sinister was smoldering in me.

"This just can't be happening," I said to myself,
I only sat in on those games that were good for my health.

Still, more tests were run, and when they came through,
It was clear that cancer was, in fact, the unlucky card that I drew.

How was this fair when I'd done everything right,
Had I not sung praises to God for my good health day and night?

Still, if the odds are against us, our best intentions can be,
A handful of illusions if they're not the ones that God sees.

So, I drew in a deep breath, and I swore I'd be strong,
As I squared off with cancer, and we took each other on.

But cancer is serious when it takes its role,
It withers the body and wilts the soul.

1

It took more from me than I thought I was willing to give,
But through the darkness, I heard my voice whisper, "I just want to live."

And live I have, thankfully, through this round of the game,
Still, with this unlucky card I hold, my life will never be the same.

So, each day, I'll place my bet since I can't change the hand I hold,
To stay high in the game of life until God says it's my time to fold.

Sandra Pickles

June 6, 2019

Introduction
The Luck of the Draw

Multiple myeloma was something I had never heard of until the latter part of June 2015. It was then that my brother-in-law, Roger, lay in a hospital bed during the last days of his life. My sister, Barbara, informed me he had been diagnosed with and treated for this relatively rare form of blood cancer in recent years.

Barbara had asked me to drive her to the hospital just a few days before his passing. Roger's oncologist stepped into the room during that visit to check on him, and Barbara introduced us. I found him to be an amiable and compassionate doctor.

Of course, at that moment, I could not have had any idea how fate would reintroduce me to this doctor again, not just once, but twice in the upcoming years, in cases relating to this deadly disease. The first being my mother's case, and the second was none other than *my own*.

Roger was 78 years old, and while this disease may not have been the only contributing factor in his passing, I assume it played its fair share of a part. My sister was twenty years his junior, and at the time, I had no idea how badly her health was failing.

In an attempt to keep the family from worrying about them, Barbara kept us in the dark about their medical conditions. That is, except for our oldest sister Jeanette, who accompanied her on many occasions to take Roger to medical facilities for various issues. Jeanette had always been the sibling caretaker, and rather than involve parents who got overly concerned and overreacted, it was our nature to reach out to her in times of crisis. Being born the first of five children, it was her nature to be mama bear. She has always looked over us all and continues to do so today.

While at the hospital, I remember Barbara saying, "no more secrets" when coming clean about their situation. She had been pretty ill and had been suffering from COPD for some time. Due to her deteriorating condition, she could not have cared for Roger alone had he left the hospital then. I was baffled as to why she told the hospital staff that she could not care for him at home by herself the day I was there with her. I tried hard to be strong for the two of them while his suffering was so apparent, and I did okay at first. He tossed and turned, moaning, as Barbara fussed over him. I could not hold back my tears, though, when he said to her, "I just want to go home." Not to their home, mind you, but home to God.

Growing up, I cried quickly, taking on my hurt feelings and feeling sorry for other people if I imagined theirs were hurt. It didn't matter whether I knew them or not. I could cry the tears of others better than they could themselves, and I was happy to oblige. I remember Barbara teasing me one day at a lunch gathering when Jeanette told us of a couple she knew who had broken up, and how heartbroken the husband was. Barbara giggled and said, "Just think, Sandra, someone else for you to feel sorry for." She, herself, was tough as nails. I ranked last in the line of my parents' five children and was always the most sensitive in the bunch. So it was natural for all the family to try to shield me from the harsh realities of life if they could since I had, and still have, a tendency to take things so hard. Especially when it comes to my family members.

Our family was not strangers to the harsh realities of life. In 1972, our sister, Linda, the second child born to my parents, died in a single-car accident. She was just seventeen years old and two and a half weeks shy of her high school graduation. My brother, Brian, had been attending the same high school as her and accepted her diploma at the graduation ceremony. I was not at that ceremony. I was eleven years old at the time, and there is so much more I remember about this tragic event than the fact that it was the hardest thing our family had ever experienced.

It wasn't many years later that Brian fell ill with bipolar disorder. He was just nineteen years old at the time and in his first semester of college.

In the months preceding my brother-in-law's passing in July 2015, our 81-year-old mother, an exceptionally energetic and exuberant woman, had gone to several doctor appointments, seeking answers for why she felt so exhausted. She had overcome pneumonia late the year before, and while her energy level had returned for a while, it eventually dipped to the point of her becoming completely exhausted. So much so that on Thanksgiving Day, when the family arrived at our parents' house for our traditional dinner celebration, she was in bed, unable to get up. My husband, Dave, and I live right around the corner from them, and we had to move the meal to our home. Dad stayed back, refusing to leave Mom alone. Her condition led to us booking more doctor appointments as we attempted to find the root cause of her fatigue.

Barbara, being all too familiar with this and other symptoms Mom described, especially after living through it with Roger, guessed Mom had multiple myeloma.

While I had not understood what this form of cancer was all about when Roger had it, it became clear once I joined Mom at her appointments and listened to what the doctors had to say. After getting in with the doctor who had treated Roger for this disease, he confirmed our mother's diagnosis: multiple myeloma.

This particular doctor did not usually take on new patients but, at Barbara's request, had agreed to see her. She had responded to his offer to let him know if there was anything he could do for her when Roger passed. He and Roger had become quite good friends during the years he treated him, especially since they both shared a love for golf. Barbara asked, "Since you lost a patient with Roger, can you take my mom on in his place?" So, he did.

Multiple myeloma is this doctor's specialty, and with his explanation in layperson's terms, I learned that this is a case where plasma cells mutate in the bone marrow, multiply, and crowd out healthy blood cells that protect the body in numerous ways. He used the example of a garden where the cancer cells are weeds that overgrow and crowd out all the other good plants growing. One of the first things I remember him saying to my mother was, "I don't see any reason why you cannot go on another ten years despite this disease."

I told my mother, "If someone told me I had the potential to live to 91, I would be pretty happy!"

So, Mom began treatments that consisted of pills and a weekly shot of a chemo drug. Dad, who loved having any reason to drive, was happy to take her back and forth to her appointments. The drive was about twenty-five miles each way. My mother eventually regained her energy and resumed her busy lifestyle. She did so well that she went off the chemo pills she'd been prescribed since they seemed to be causing her excessive itching.

At some point in this same year, after visiting my doctor for my annual physical, I got an unusual result on my blood tests. I expected my doctor to say, "Everything looks great; you are healthier than anybody has a right to be." Those were the exact words he had used to describe my blood test results from the previous year. This time, however, he said, "Things look good, other than your white blood cell count was lower than before." He was not overly concerned about this, but said he would want to keep an eye on it. Since he was not concerned, I wasn't either.

However, I was disappointed that I wasn't healthier than anybody had a right to be. After all, I took great pride in my healthy lifestyle and the fact that I was very rarely ever sick. When I was under the weather, my recovery time was rapid. Like my mother's, my energy level was through the roof, and I was constantly moving. The thought that there was anything to be seriously concerned about regarding my health was the furthest thing from my mind. If it related to me, any health concern couldn't mean much. How could anything be wrong with me when I always felt so good?

Come 2016; my white blood count dipped even lower. While there are numerous causes for low white blood counts, knowing the reason in a specific case is not always obvious. In one conversation with my doctor's nurse, she said, "While your white blood cell count continues to go lower than average, this may be normal for you."

That was a weak hypothesis for my husband and me as well.

Chapter One

Diagnosis

I'm unclear when my doctor eventually became concerned enough to refer me to an oncologist. I was unaware that oncology was the study of cancer at that time. Therefore, I had no reason to panic or be overly concerned when my doctor suggested this. There is some truth to the saying, "Ignorance is bliss." I felt a little better when my husband admitted that he didn't know it then either.

The first question the oncologist asked me when I met with her was, "How old were your parents when they passed?" She was delighted when I told her they were still with us and in their eighties. I let her know right away that my mother had been diagnosed with multiple myeloma some time back. She was not initially concerned about this, saying this disease wasn't ordinarily hereditary. We ran blood tests, and she prescribed iron supplements. Life went on as usual for me, and I had no particular sense of concern.

The following tests showed *too much* iron in my blood, so I was taken off those supplements and put on some form of Vitamin B.

On went the testing and monitoring, and I grew more frustrated with taking time out of my busy schedule to have blood drawn. Then, in a separate appointment, I met with the oncologist for five minutes for a conversation that resulted in more questions than answers. I needed help.

Around this time, I recall making a remark to Dave about my low white blood cell count in the presence of our teenage son, Tyler. We had not discussed this around him before, and his instant response was, "Well, that's not good." Tyler is an intelligent student and is interested in the sciences. At that moment, it occurred to me that maybe I should be taking this more seriously.

When my next annual checkup came about with my primary doctor, he had another set of labs ordered. His nurse called me and said, "Your white blood cell count is now the lowest since we started monitoring it in 2015." I didn't even know what year this had initially become a concern, and that statement was the only hint to me of when my white blood cell counts had started dropping in the first place. This finding resulted in my oncologist referring me for a bone marrow biopsy in September 2017.

Though not something to look forward to, I was again more frustrated at having more time taken away from my busy work schedule than I was about any results this test may produce. This biopsy would be a time-consuming procedure, and Dave took the day off work to take me. This process occurred at a hospital next to the clinic where my mother went to get her cancer treatments. Again, roughly twenty-five miles each way. It was, of course, somewhat unpleasant. The biopsy was done with anesthesia, but with a high tolerance for pain medication, I felt everything. Dave's support was a blessing, and we finished up and went home.

Strangely enough, I still don't recall being so concerned that I lost any sleep over the whole situation. There were too many other things going on in my life that held my attention. I was still reeling from the loss of my father less than four months before this time, and I was also in the latter stages of completing a year-long management program at work. To say I was obsessed with work and this program would be a major understatement.

When the oncologist's office called to schedule an appointment to review the biopsy, I didn't expect the results. It never occurred to me to have my husband join me for the meeting planned for the morning of October 3rd, 2017, and my doctor didn't suggest it either. I rushed to get in and out of there as quickly as possible and return to work. After all, an all-staff meeting was scheduled for the following morning, and we, management trainees, would highlight the program in front of all those employed by the financial institution I worked for. I wanted nothing more than to be back at work, perfecting my part in the presentation.

My oncologist and a young lady whom she was mentoring and whom I had met during my last appointment entered the room where I was waiting. Without a greeting, the doctor walked toward me, dropped a stack of papers on the table in front of me, and said, "Well, we found something we didn't want to see. You may be following in the footsteps of your mother. We believe you may have the same thing she does."

I knew she had to be talking about Mom's cancer.

My first response was, "So, are you telling me I only have ten years to live?"

That was from the impression made by my mother's doctor when he told her he saw no reason she could not go on another ten years, despite having this disease. Still, Mom was 81 when she was diagnosed, and I had just turned fifty-seven less than three weeks before this time. Sixty-seven didn't sound near as favorable an expectation, and I was already very well aware that there is no cure for multiple myeloma.

The doctor shook her head hard at my inquiry, firmly emphasizing that she had said nothing of the sort. She said, "Many treatments are available today, and promising research is underway for future therapies. No one knows what may be available in ten years," she added. At this stage of the game, she hoped it might be smoldering myeloma, a precursor to multiple myeloma, which is not quite as severe. She could not know for sure until she had bone scans and more blood tests. She said if it were, in fact, multiple myeloma, she would recommend I undergo a stem cell transplant, which would require me to be in the hospital for a month.

"Are you kidding me?" I asked. "I can't spend a month in the hospital."

If I had known then how easy a month in the hospital would have been compared to how things turned out, I would have had good reason to be thankful on that day. I didn't know, though, and following my initial reaction of shock and disbelief to the news given me that morning, I felt anger. I had built my life around a healthy lifestyle. I ate right (or so I thought), worked out hard three or more times a week at the gym, walked my dog twice a day, and kept a positive mental attitude. *How in the world could there be anything seriously wrong with me? What happened to me being healthier than anybody had a right to be?*

After providing me orders for more extensive blood tests, and one for a bone scan at our local hospital, I was given a follow-up appointment with her a month out. *A month?* That is a long time to wait for answers about something as serious as cancer. Though more time away from work that morning was not enticing, it made sense to get my ducks in a row quickly to get this all out of the way. After leaving with my orders, I drove directly to the lab to see how long a wait there might be for a blood draw.

Luck was on my side at the diagnostic lab. Not one person was in the waiting room when I arrived, and I was in and out of there in minutes.

I had previously scheduled some unrelated medical appointments but needed to know the dates and times. Again, these were inconveniences in my mind, unimportant things I needed to be more organized in documenting. Having decided to check on the dates and times of those commitments so I could schedule an appointment for a bone scan, I drove directly home from the lab.

After confirming that information, I dialed my husband at work. Calling him there was a rare occurrence, but it was still early in the day, and I didn't feel I could wait until the end of the day to talk to him about all this. When I got him on the line and told him that the oncologist said I might have the same thing my mom has, there was a moment of silence on the other end, after which he said, "Kind of makes you want to light up a cigarette and pop open a beer, doesn't it?"

Relieved at his attempt at humor, I laughed a little and replied, "Yeah, it kind of does."

Smoking was a habit I'd quit twenty-six years before this time, after a sixteen-plus-year practice. Quitting that habit was one of the hardest things I have ever done. It was also one of my proudest accomplishments in my quest for good health.

"So," Dave reiterated, "they think you might have what your mom has, huh? I thought multiple myeloma was rare and not hereditary," he said.

"I thought so, too," I replied. Then, after a brief silence, I said, "Well, it picked the wrong person." I was still furious about the diagnosis given me, and after telling Dave I would talk to him when we both got home, I called the local hospital, got my bone scan scheduled, and then went back to work.

Once there, I took my usual seat in the office of my management mentor and tried to take my mind off what had just transpired. My mood was somber, and he asked me how things went. Knowing he was referring to my doctor's appointment, I felt it only fair to be honest with him. Not just out of respect for our friendship, but he had also volunteered for three months of training on my behalf. He deserved to know why there may be more time I needed for doctor's appointments during the last month of the program.

Asking that he keep it to himself, I explained what the doctor had told me. He offered me any support he could provide and encouraged me to take whatever time I needed for appointments.

Work was a sanctuary where I could keep my mind busy and escape the realities of my problems. It kept me from dwelling on life for years, and I depended on it far too much for that. When my father passed on a Monday morning, I exited a staff meeting without explanation after getting a call from my mother. I later sent my boss a text, apologizing for my abrupt exit, informing him that my father had passed and that I would not be in the office the following day.

When he came into the office Wednesday morning and found me at my desk, he came over and asked, "What are you doing here?"

I told him I didn't want to sit at home alone and dwell on things.

He said, "No, seriously, what are you doing here?"

I had no other explanation. He suggested I go back home. Being home was the last place I wanted to be, so I chose to stay. As it turned out, my stay there that morning was short-lived, as after a couple of hours, I received a call from my mother informing me she had been involved in a car accident and was in the hospital. She had run a stop sign while in town, and someone hit her. She was the only one who required medical attention, and her car was totaled. I immediately left work and went to the hospital, where I was involved with more stressful family issues for the rest of the day.

So, the remainder of the workday on October 3rd passed. Everyone was excited about the big employee meeting scheduled for the following morning. My mind turned over and over as I silently practiced the lines I would say during my part of our presentation. The meeting was at a site different from where these events usually took place, and being that I had only been there once, I needed to figure out how to get there. The route was confusing to me the first time I went, and I had been a passenger rather than the driver during that trip. That I would be driving there alone this time only added to my anxiety. My best hope was that I would spot a coworker on the way and be able to follow them there.

I can't recall much of the conversation between Dave and me when we got home from work the day my oncologist shared that news. We couldn't know what we'd be facing without complete confirmation of the diagnosis. My bone scan would take place within the next couple of days, and we hoped for more answers once we got those results and those of my last blood draw. In the meantime, we tried to be as hopeful as possible that they would come back as smoldering rather than multiple myeloma. While it would not be good news, it would be somewhat less severe.

The following morning, I left the house to head to our meeting. I did luck out on spotting an employee from the branch I worked at and followed her there. I practiced my script all the way there. The event went great. I remembered my lines and even got a laugh out of the audience in my deliverance. The entire group did great, and we congratulated ourselves and each other for "killing it." I was in my element. Still, concern about the news handed to me the day before was nagging at the back of my brain.

As in any event, life continues, and Dave and I hoped for the best. Not wanting to say anything to anybody else at this time, we kept things to ourselves. I soon went to the local hospital for my bone scan. The radiologist who did the scan was training two young interns, and in her step-by-step demonstration of the process, she explained to them how the images would pick up cancer. My senses clouded, and my confused mind repeatedly asked itself, "I have cancer? … I have cancer?"

There was no denying the possibility, but I couldn't come to terms with the fact that she was referring to me. With the scan completed, I dressed to leave. One of the young women who had helped with the protocol during the procedure walked outside with me. She advised me to do my best to be around positive people and think happy thoughts. She said to eat soup made with bone marrow and lots of vegetables. She told me her boyfriend had low white blood counts also and had for some time, but he refused to have further testing done to find out why. I encouraged her to continue trying to persuade him to get more answers. I truly appreciated her taking the time to talk to me, and I hoped her boyfriend would get tested sooner rather than later for her peace of mind as well as his. I thanked her for her time and went back to work.

All this took place in early October, and it seemed so many things in my personal life were going wrong. My mother had left for Oregon at the very end of September to see her two sisters and would be gone almost the whole month of October. I had no intention of giving her any of this news over the phone and ruining her trip. Especially with recently losing Dad, the stress of the car accident just two days after that, which her injured back was healing from, and the never-ending things one has to do paperwork-wise when someone passes. She deserved this time to be happy. So, until I could tell her in person, I didn't want anyone else to know, not even Dave's family. He is one of seven children, and the family is exceptionally close.

I did share my situation with my siblings. I called Barbara, making small talk and trying to think about how to bring up this news. Once she said she had to go take care of something, I panicked and said there was something I had to tell her. As best I could, I told her what the doctor had told me.

She was shocked and just kept saying, "Aww shit, aww shit." She asked if I had talked with Jeanette about this.

I told her, "No, but would you mind if I try to get the three of us together on a conference call?"

She said, "Okay."

I felt that I had to come to clean immediately with both my big sisters simultaneously so I wouldn't get in trouble. I was able to get Jeanette in on the call and explained to her what was going on. She was shocked as well. "Oh boy," she said. A silence then hung on the line, after which she said again, in that foreboding tone, "Oh boy."

The three of us talked awhile, and Barbara wondered if she could call the nurse of the doctor who had treated Roger and was currently treating our mother to see what the chances were of him agreeing to see me. The idea appealed to me, as he seemed to be so personable with my mother and Roger.

A second opinion would be excellent, and our conversation ended with the understanding that Barbara would reach out to this doctor's nurse the following day. I also spoke with my brother to make him aware, but he was going through one of his manic stages and could not comprehend the seriousness of what I was sharing with him. His condition was more stressful to me than my own. It was especially concerning since Mom was out of state and not around to take care of him should someone need to. I felt the added concern of staying in touch with him and trying to keep him from going over the deep end.

Chapter Two
A Second Opinion

Over the next few days, Barbara spoke with the nurse at my mother's doctor's office, and she asked Barbara to have me call their office and make an appointment. I did, and the nurse instructed me to have my oncologist forward them a copy of my medical records. I spoke with the receptionist, who asked if this was for a second opinion or a transfer of care. I told her it was for a second opinion. Within the next few days, that same receptionist called me back to move my appointment with them, which had been scheduled for a month out, to the following week.

Dave and I went together and discussed the results of the bone scan and my last blood test with my oncologist. The scan showed no damage to the bones; however, the blood work showed those missing markers, confirming that what I had was indeed multiple myeloma. This was a terrible blow that I'm not sure we were willing to accept until we got a second opinion. We let the doctor know we would be in touch.

The date for my appointment with my mother's oncologist came, and Dave and I waited together in the doctor's office. The doctor came rushing in with a big smile, looking at us, and immediately asked, "Hasn't there already been enough multiple myeloma in this family?"

We laughed a little, wholeheartedly agreeing. This was supposed to be a relatively rare form of cancer, yet it had struck three members of my family in recent years, though Roger was not blood-related. Based on what he saw from my records and my local oncologist's office test results, his diagnosis was the same as hers. I did, in fact, have multiple myeloma. He still wanted to see the results of a twenty-four-hour yearn test and get authorization from my insurance company to order a pet scan. This is a much more detailed set of images of the bones and internal organs prone to damage by this disease. So, we prepared for that.

We continued to keep our news to ourselves, though some friends could tell something was wrong. Dave tried so hard to help me believe things were going to be okay, as we spent that month feeling like we were living in a bad dream. I did not want to leave my bed in the morning for the entire month of October. This is completely opposite of how I usually am, as I love mornings. I love to get up before dawn each day to drink my coffee and thank God for all the good things He has given me.

First and foremost, I thanked Him for the good health I was so proud of and worked so hard at. Now, I felt so betrayed by Him and my own body that I had no desire to get up. Nor did I have anything to say to God at this particular time. I was afraid of what I would say if I did get out of bed and take my usual spot there on the couch with Him and my coffee. Maybe a sarcastic, "Hey there … yeah … thanks for this." I knew that none of this was God's fault any more than mine. Still, I felt if anyone could have prevented this from happening in the first place, it certainly would have been Him. So why didn't He? I also knew, though, that if anyone could get me through this, even if what I have can't be cured, it would be God.

I am still not sure how we survived that traumatic month of October. So much seemed to be going wrong in our lives—the shock of this news, the concern about my brother's spiraling mental health, and not having my mother around to talk to. Dave's brother's 18-year-old nephew by marriage went missing, and the personal effects he left behind hinted at suicide. A couple of weeks later, a body would be found at the bottom of a mountain in their local area, and the grim identification process would begin. It would, in fact, turn out to be him. We were heartbroken for his family and the troubled soul that left this earth at such a young age.

I was also six or seven weeks into a sixteen-week computer class at our local community college, which was so stressful that I am traumatized by it to this day. The course covered three software programs and a section that dove into hardware, wiring, and other bits of information that were Greek to me. Still, I refused to drop it.

The class met just once a week, and if you had questions in the interim, you had to email the teacher. Trying to word a question to email the teacher on paper was more time-consuming and complicated than figuring things out for myself. I would shut myself up in our home office for hours, struggling to get through this course.

During this trying time, even our poor dog, who never had health issues, was suffering terribly from skin and flea issues which required vet visits, multiple medications, and extra care. I felt terrible for him.

To make matters worse, my mother called me from Oregon to ask if we had heard the news that Santa Rosa, California, where much of her family lived and where we had lived for a year in 1965 while my father served in Vietnam, was going up in flames. I did not know. This was the 2017 Tubbs Fire, which burned more than 34,000 acres and was responsible for the deaths of thirteen people.

Mom informed me that the beloved "Old Red Barn," which had been located behind my grandparents' motel, had burned to the ground. The barn was a landmark and held many memories for all the grandkids on my mother's side, as we played inside it as kids. It was also the subject of one of the poems I had written in the late 1980s. That barn, standing or burned to the ground, will always be near and dear to my heart. This was devastating news, and the conversation between my mother and me continued while I tried to sound like life was normal on the home front. I could not bring myself to share anything with her about my health condition, and it tore me up inside to hear her voice and know the news that awaited her when she got home.

"The Old Red Barn"

The Old Red Barn sat atop of a hill,
Behind Grandma's house out across a field.
Three stories high is what they said it stood,
With its red paint a peelin' and its old rotting wood.

Surrounded by brush and a faint smell of sage,
We kids were warned not to play there because of its age.
But with that sense of adventure, which no child can ignore,
We would all run up that hill to The Old Red Barn and explore.

And we would each watch our footing every step of the way,
As we passed through the door into darkness from the broad light of day.
And it was there in the embrace of those creaky old walls,
That the forgotten world of yesterday would open to us all.

Amongst the cobwebs on the walls, upon rusty nails we'd see,
Old ropes and pails and hay receipts, showing hints of history.
The shovels, rakes, and baling wire, the broken boards of withered stalls,
Kept us wondering if the ghost of some farmer didn't live here after all.

Well, there was never any end to the discoveries that were made,
As we crept about those gloomy corners where our imaginations strayed.
Yet there was a place we could never reach, built high above the rest,
That was the peak of the rounded roof and the home of the pigeon's nest.

Still, we could live out any fantasy here, for every child knew,
There lurked some magic in the old barn that made each one come true.
Yes, the thought of the Old Red Barn at Grandma's house will always give,
A reminder of the past and places where our childhood memories still live.

Sandra R. Pickles

May 27, 1987

October 31st would conclude the three months with my mentor in a department different from where I usually worked, and finishing strong was so important to me. Monday through Friday, I went to work each morning with a smile and acted like I didn't have a care in the world other than to be the best manager-in-training anyone could ever be. Again, to say I was obsessed with work was an understatement.

I graduated with a bachelor's degree in sociology in 2006. While shelving my pursuit of career advancement for years, I began to revisit the idea when the manager of the department I worked in announced his plan to depart. Our son, Tyler, had graduated high school four months before this time, and this management program and possible career advancement would be the perfect remedy for what I assumed would soon be empty nest syndrome.

Was I ready to move up? No. After being given false hope for quite some time by the departing manager, the VP who oversaw my area sat me down. He said while he appreciated my efforts in unofficially leading the department I worked in during the absence of a manager and applying for the open manager position, I needed more time to be ready. He promised that this was where the management training program would come in, and it would help me become prepared. That said, he looked me in the eye and asked if I was okay.

I said, "Yes, I'm fine."

This conversation took place in the latter part of 2016, and now, October 2017 would conclude that year-long training program. It had been a lot of hard work. We presented speeches, took online courses, and were tested on what we learned from them. We were required to attend community events, and we showed up at our monthly meetings decked out in slick business attire while we prepared for what we hoped would be a chance at moving up into a managerial position. Navigating the online courses was my biggest challenge due to my lack of computer skills, and I often wanted to scream in frustration, begging my computer-competent son to come in and help me. Somehow, I got through it.

I loved learning and being part of a like-minded group of coworkers. I also cherished the camaraderie and the friendships that developed between us in the program that still carry on today. My fellow students would later become part of my support system.

A couple of our human resources department employees and the assistant vice president of our financial institution taught the course. This person had sat me down for the previously noted conversation about my need to better prepare for a management role. We appreciated their time and training during working hours, though there were times one of our teachers was absent as she was battling cancer.

She did ask us during some of our meetings if we would be offended if she removed the hat covering her head since she was bald.

"Of course not," we would answer. I am sure the others admired her as much as I for her dignity and determination as she lifted and set that veil aside. We were so hopeful the remission she was in would last. It was not to be. After some promising progress, we learned that she was once again on medical leave, and donations of paid time off from other employees on her behalf would be appreciated. I donated eighty hours, as I'm sure many others did. At the time, I had so much paid time off accrued I was in a "use it or lose it" status.

Sadly, before our program ended, we would learn that this person passed at home with her husband by her side. She had slipped away while the two of them sat listening to her favorite songs. It was devastating to us all, especially for her HR counterpart, who was one of our three teachers. Not only were they coworkers, but the two of them had also become very close friends. She emailed all the staff on a Saturday morning about her passing. This took place before my diagnosis, and I felt at that time, as most of us do, that only "other people" get cancer.

So, on went this very dark month. Two oncologists confirmed that I had multiple myeloma, and both recommended I undergo a stem cell transplant following several months of weekly chemo shots in conjunction with an oral chemo pill taken three weeks on and one week off. I was in a quandary over whether I would stay with my local oncologist or transfer my care to the doctor who had taken care of my brother-in-law and continued overseeing my mother's care. Staying local, of course, would mean less time taken off work for me. Still, my husband and sisters encouraged me to go with my mother's doctor. This particular type of cancer is his specialty, and he worked at a cancer center with much more to offer besides treatments than my local oncologist's office did. I asked my mother's doctor if I could work out doing shots and oral medications under my local doctor's care while also under his care.

He didn't feel my local oncologist would agree to that. Once he confirmed he would permanently take me as a patient, I called my local oncologist's office and asked the receptionist to provide all my records to him for transfer of care.

The time was approaching for my mother to come home from Oregon, and I dreaded the conversation we would soon have. But at least I had accepted the reality of my situation and emerged from the dark to reclaim my time in the morning and my daily cups of coffee with God. I am a person who will stress out so hard over something for some time and then get to a point where I am completely done with it. Though I knew I would never be done with this incurable cancer, I was tired of stressing out and feeling sorry for myself. It was time to get on with life. I was going to have multiple myeloma, whether happy or sad, so I chose happy and defiant.

Chapter Three
A Temporary Setback

I was determined that all this would not bring me down, change who I was, or change my plans. This would be a temporary setback in my path, nothing more. Right? In those days, I truly believed that. I was fifty-seven, and it had taken me until now to get to a place where I felt there may be some reality in my chances to advance in my job after thirty years of employment there, and nothing was going to stop me now. That was then, though, and this is now.

Mom came home in the latter part of October, and on the Saturday following her arrival, I prepared myself to prepare her. As I mentioned, Dave and I live right around the corner from my parents' family home, but the 191-foot walk there that morning felt like a hundred miles on my heart.

She was expecting me and had the garage door opened so I could enter through it without her having to get up. She sat on the couch in her slippers and robe, enjoying a cup of coffee. She felt good to be home, and I took a seat across from her.

"Mom, I have something to share with you, which isn't good news."

She looked at me and asked, "What?"

I asked if she remembered me telling her about the low white blood counts my doctor had been concerned about; she nodded, her eyes wide now with concern.

I said, "It seems I have multiple myeloma, too, and will need to undergo a stem cell transplant."

Her head slowly sunk to the back cushion of the couch as her eyes closed, and I watched as her anguish drained the color from her face. My chest hurt as I felt my heart break for her.

In trying to make it sound not quite so bad, I explained that this was caught early and the pet scan had shown no damage to my bones or internal organs. It still took a few minutes for her to be able to speak. She and I then spent some time visiting before I gathered myself, hugged her, and headed home. I told her I did not want this news in the Christmas letter she sent to family and friends every year.

Glad to have that behind me, I went home, told Dave how it went, and told him he could now share our situation with his family. We also shared the news with a couple of our close friends. They were shocked.

Dave and I had plans to meet a few of his siblings and their spouses for dinner one evening shortly after that, and at this point, I could talk openly about it to them in a matter-of-fact manner while being optimistic about what was to come. My sister-in-law, Jill, had once told me that I was the most positive person she knew, and I wanted to remain that person.

On November 1st, I reported back to my assigned department at work. The three-month mentee period of the steps program was over, and while I had told my mentor of my condition, we had not discussed it any further. The employees in his department celebrated my completion of the time with them with gifts, a little party, and well wishes. We had all become quite close.

The vice president of the collections department and I had also bonded upon his arrival. I had been a part of introducing him in, and he knew of my efforts to keep things together before leadership found someone to manage us. He was generous in his efforts to help me progress in a managerial direction. He was delighted when I was selected as a participant in the program, cheering me on along the way. Now I needed to go into his office and tell him about my situation.

I took a deep breath, and as my friend and I often said to each other when we had to deal with something challenging, put my big girl panties on. I put my phone on an "away from desk" status and walked to his office. It was early, and we were the only ones in the department. Standing at his door, I asked if he had a minute, and when he said, "Yes," I stepped in, closed the door behind me in case anyone else entered the department, and took a seat facing him. I told him of my diagnosis and the potential need for time out of the office for treatment. I also explained I might soon be out an entire month for a stem cell transplant.

He was as shocked as others had been upon hearing this news for the first time. He assured me that whatever time I needed was mine without question. There was no way for him to express how sorry he was to hear all this, and I felt sorry for him as his face flushed red (remember, I felt sorry for everyone); after all, what do you say to someone who sits down facing you, looks you in the eye, and tells you they have cancer? It couldn't be pleasant. He advised me to schedule a meeting with our human resources department to notify them of my situation and gather as much information as possible regarding leave and disability. Somehow, the thought of needing to do this made my situation more real. He did forewarn me to expect a reaction to the news from our vice president of human resources since we had recently lost her counterpart to cancer. He also suggested that I not share this news with the rest of the team to avoid spreading unnecessary fear. I had no intentions or desire to share my situation, so I was more than happy to oblige.

Soon I met with our HR representative, gave her the news, and asked for guidance on leave. The first thing this person said to me, after saying how sorry she was to hear of my condition, was that I looked like I was ready to fight. I assured her I was.

I had a lot of paid time off banked already, so that would play in my favor. We went over different options for when that time ran out, but it was all too overwhelming for me to understand. I left that meeting more confused than when I walked in. I had never had to consider disability, and truth be told, I was still in denial that needing to understand it related to me in the first place. In my mind, disability was only there for "other people."

At least now, the ball was rolling there concerning what was happening with my health.

Shortly after that, I ran into the VP, who was one of our teachers in the management program I had completed. This being the same person who had recommended the program to me, saw me and walked over to talk to me. HR had made him aware of my condition, as he was the assistant vice president of the financial institution I worked for and oversaw my department. He said he was sorry to hear of my condition and that his wife had it too. I was speechless for a moment. Finally, I looked at him and asked, "Multiple myeloma?"

He said, "No, breast cancer."

I told him how sorry I was to hear that and asked that he keep me posted on her condition and her progress in fighting it.

Soon after that, I entered the lady's room and ran into the HR person who had been close friends with the employee who had recently succumbed to cancer. She stood speechless, looking at me with a fallen face and tears in her eyes. I took her hands in mine, my eyes holding hers, and said, "I am going to be okay."

She somewhat crumbled, saying how shocked and sorry she was to learn of my diagnosis. I squeezed her hands tighter and, this time with more conviction, said, "I am going to be okay." And I meant it. I had not, and still have not, allowed myself to shed a tear over my disease.

Somewhere deep inside, I believe, passed down to me by my father, lies a streak of stubborn pride, and I refused to let my cancer make me cry. Had it been someone else, I would be bawling, but to show sorrow in the face of my own fate was to let cancer think it had in some way won, and I refused to give in to that. I was angry, shocked, and saddened, which is to be expected, but I couldn't understand why I felt so ashamed of myself. Like this was somehow my fault and that I was now less of a person.

I would walk past people with my eyes cast down and glance up at them, my thoughts taunting me with a whisper that asked, "Do they know?"

Was this cancer bestowed upon me because I was a horrible human being? Had I done something so wrong that I deserved all this?

Shortly after being diagnosed, I dreamed of walking with my mother across the field in front of the housing area of the Air Force Base where we had lived in the 1970s. We were on our way to a women's detention center where I was being sent, I assume to serve time for the crime of having cancer. When we arrived, and the women in the facility saw me, they started backing away from me, putting as much distance between themselves and me as possible, obviously concerned that I would contaminate them with my disease.

The woman in charge stood before me, holding two loofah sponges, one in each hand, both the size of an angel's wings. She told me to go shower—as if I could wash this filthy disease off my body. I went in search of an available shower, finding the curtain drawn and hearing the water running behind each one I approached. Amidst the steam rising up from behind each drawn curtain and the sound of water running in my ears, my search continued as the dream faded to an end.

Back at work, I carried on each day, working as hard as possible to keep my mind busy and off my problems. It was my escape from this problem, too. The more that life happened, the deeper I drove myself into my job and career growth. I liked being thought of as the department's go-to girl, and I didn't want to relinquish that role.

My treatments were scheduled to start in the latter part of November. Before this, Dave and I were scheduled to meet with the cancer center's social worker. She provided me with a notebook of information on what we could expect with what we were about to go through and what we could do to make it somewhat easier for us. The first thing she said to me when we sat down was how important it was to know that this was not my fault, "It's just the luck of the draw," she said. She told us her husband's late wife had had multiple myeloma but lived fully to the end every day of her life.

Maybe not exactly what I wanted to hear at the moment ... but ... okay.

She informed me that steroids would also become part of my treatment, and if I had problems sleeping now (which I did and had been having for many years), wait till those kicked in.

Great!!

She said I should use an electric razor rather than a regular one to avoid nicks and cuts when shaving my legs and underarms, as I would be prone to heavy bleeding due to cancer and the medications I was on. My immune system was now suppressed and could no longer be counted on to fight infection.

"Really?" I thought. I am fifty-seven and have been shaving my legs with a razor since I was, oh, maybe twelve. This cancer was taking over my body and my way of life.

This meeting lasted forty-five minutes to an hour. I tried to pay as close attention as I could, but I was so hungry I couldn't wait to leave so we could go eat. Finally, we left and went to have breakfast at a restaurant nearby.

There were a lot of people sitting in the waiting area where we were seated, and I overheard a woman talking on her cell phone. Her conversation led me to believe she had just left a meeting worse than the one we had just sat through, as I heard her say, "He told her, 'We are all going to die; you're just going to die a little sooner.' What kind of a thing is that to say to a kid?" she asked whomever it was that was on the other end of the line.

I couldn't believe what I was hearing and tried to focus my attention elsewhere. We finally got seated and ordered our meal. At least the food was good, and I did feel somewhat better afterward.

So began my regimen of oral chemo pills, accompanied by weekly shots every Tuesday afternoon. Dave asked my doctor if the treatments would cause my hair to fall out. I was a fanatic about the appearance of my hair, so we were both relieved when the doctor said, "No, it shouldn't."

Every Tuesday, I left the office early to go home and meet Dave so he could take me for my shot. Each time I pushed leaving up to and past the very last minute. I always tried to get one more thing done, causing us to rush and Dave to get very frustrated with me. The shots were given in the back of my upper arm, and each time, it left an angry red spot at the injection site. I'm a person who runs warm and usually wears sleeveless or short-sleeved clothing to stay comfortable. Now, I had to adjust my wardrobe and comfort level by wearing long sleeves to hide these marks. I didn't want anyone asking me to explain where those red marks came from.

When a coworker got curious enough to ask what I was doing every Tuesday when I left early, I blew it off as needing to do chores. When conversations came up between my coworkers related to customers or acquaintances being diagnosed with or having passed from cancer, I didn't bat an eye. My stubborn pride kept me from entertaining any illusions that I could be the next one they discussed between them, so I simply stayed out of the conversations.

We live in a small community, and most of my family members do their banking at the financial institution I worked at. I sometimes worried that one of them would mention my situation to one of the employees as they did their banking, as we had not sworn anyone to secrecy. However, there is only so much one can worry about at one time, and I already had enough on my plate to contemplate. I couldn't dwell on possibilities.

Once treatment started, my oncologist suggested I wear a mask at work or request my own office. Though I knew the treatments, on top of the low white blood cell count, made me even more suscep-tible to illnesses, I couldn't conceive of making such adjustments. No way could I ask someone in upper management to give up their office for me.

My disease was still incognito, and doing that or wearing a mask would have been a dead giveaway to my situation.

Chapter Four

Incognito

I couldn't even accept that I should limit my exposure to crowds. I look forward to the company's holiday party every year, and there was no way this year would be different. I just love to dance, and this was one of the few opportunities I got to do so. I wasn't going to miss it. It is also a tradition for Dave and me to stay the night at the hotel where the party is held, some forty-five miles away, and have breakfast the following day at a restaurant nearby. So, we went to the party to dine, dance, and celebrate. If anyone there had asked me if I had cancer, I would have answered, "Not tonight, I don't." I was careful to limit my alcohol intake, and life was good for the moment.

One day during the week following that party, I was returning to my office after lunch. Hearing my name being called from behind me as I made my way down the hall, I turned around. Our CEO stood outside the door of his office area, looking at me, and I made my way back to where he was standing. He said a little birdie told him I was having some health issues and wanted to know how I was doing. I told him of my circumstances and how the month of October had been a very dark one for me. He said his wife had been upset with him at the holiday party for not asking me how I was doing. He said he'd told her, "I didn't know." It felt good to know I could be open with him about my situation while not being overly concerned he would share it with others.

December continued with its usual events, and 2017 came to a close. Dave and I spent New Year's Eve with friends and family at a club nearby, where we had celebrated in years past. Another opportunity for me to dance, and I was in good spirits. There, we saw a friend of ours who had been my boss at the financial institution I worked for and with whom I had developed a close friendship before his retirement. He and his wife are special to Dave and me, and we shared our situation with them. They were shocked and so very concerned. He felt I shouldn't be working, or at the least, should be wearing a mask if I was. I just have to work was my reply to him. It was inconceivable to me not to. I promised to be careful, and we entered 2018.

Life was full of adjustments, treatments, and frustration trying to sort through the healthcare system. You can only ever seem to talk to the same representative once when you call, and every person gives you a different answer to your questions, along with a new set of rules to follow. Getting monthly refills on my oral chemo medication was an ordeal in and of itself. Each month required a fifteen-to-twenty-minute phone conversation with someone at a specialty pharmacy in another state.

Finding any privacy to speak with them during the workday was challenging, and their offices were closed when I was off. Trying to converse with them before I reported to work often led me to be on my cell phone on the drive there, which I didn't want to be doing. All this for someone who, in the past, had no place in her life for inconveniences such as these. I was thankful that Dave was much more organized and persistent in reaching out to our insurance providers for information and scheduling appointments for the tests I would require before the transplant.

One day, as Dave and I got out of the car and headed into the cancer center for my doctor's appointment, he once again said, "I still can't believe we are coming here on your behalf and that you have cancer."

It was surreal to me too, and I wanted to change the subject or make light of it each time he said it. I already felt guilty enough for causing so much trouble, and maybe I thought I could make the truth disappear by not focusing on it. "I can't believe it either," was my response in somewhat of a nonchalant tone, but I do.

I guess he wanted my frustration to go beyond his since it was my body this was happening to, but my attitude must not have been what he was hoping for. In his frustration, he exclaimed, "Sandra, this cancer is in your blood. Doesn't that bother you?"

"Well, of course, it bothers me," I said, "but what do you want me to do? I have it; I can't do anything about that. I'm going to have it whether I'm happy or sad, and I'll be damned if I'm going to waste whatever time I have left in life moping around about it."

This same type of conversation also occurred between my mother and me one day when I was driving the two of us somewhere. I got the impression that she, too, felt like I was not taking all this as seriously as I should be. What else did they want me to do? I saw my doctor regularly, got my blood drawn every month, got my shots every week, and took my oral medication as directed.

Depression was not something I wanted to add to the mix. I loved being happy-go-lucky, and besides, I'd wallowed away enough time after being diagnosed in October, and I was done with it. I didn't always know how to deal with my feelings and fears about what was happening in my body. Still, I wanted to be as positive about life as possible.

I became able to recognize the feelings of my own reactions to those sometimes-overwhelming fears and knew my own remedies for distracting my mind and, in many cases, controlling my mood.

What I couldn't know, or of course control, was how my loved ones felt about these things, when they were thinking about them, or how they handled their emotions. Nor could I know how deep their sorrows were or what they did to distract their minds from their fears. It wasn't just me enduring the consequences of this disease; I bear the guilt of inflicting them on those I love who love me, too. It is a horribly helpless feeling to know you are the root of other people's pain and that, try as you might, you cannot calm their emotions as you may be able to your own.

It was also frustrating that I could fix what was happening outside my body but could not help what was happening inside it. When I was a smoker, I physically controlled that habit. I decided to put those cigarettes to my lips and inhale their poison. I continued making that decision for a long time.

I also, though, made the decision to quit. I wanted to stop the effects it was having on my body inside and out and end my addiction. A friend of mine and I were having a conversation one day while we were out horseback riding about my having smoked for a long time, giving it up numerous times, only to go back to it again and again before finally calling it quits once and for all. She asked what made me ultimately decide to let it go for good. I told her I couldn't stand the fact that something had more control over my body than I did. It was my body, and I wanted to take back what belonged to me, so I did.

While it was one of the hardest things I have ever done, it also was one of the most necessary, not just for my physical health but for my mental health as well.

When you have an incurable form of cancer, you cannot control the decision to quit, mentally or physically. You can't even mediate. I don't know what is happening inside my body from one moment to the next. I have to rely on blood and urine tests, pet scans, and bone marrow biopsies to tell me what is going on inside me at any given time. Then, I have to rely on a doctor to explain all those results to me in a language that is, naturally, hard for me to comprehend. It is such a helpless feeling to not only not know but to not be able to slow down, stop or control the war that's taking place inside you. A body that used to belong to you, but is now controlled by a deadly disease. So, as you can imagine, there is almost always a level of apprehension when we attend my monthly doctor appointments to learn the results of my most recent labs and what they will tell us about how this monster is behaving or misbehaving.

The cancer center I go to continuously offers a variety of complimentary classes and lectures to its patients and their caregivers. One course in particular that appealed to me was "Look good, feel better." This is a class where the instructor would demonstrate to women how to downplay cancer's adverse side effects on their appearance by using makeup and shading techniques to brighten their faces. They would also show us how to utilize wigs and scarves for dressing up our outfits and boost our confidence. Cute and colorful garments can be wrapped or tied around one's head or neck in various fun and attractive ways. They serve as great tools for those suffering from cancer, especially for those women who are bald or whose hair is thinning due to chemo.

As obsessed as I have always been about my hair and makeup, I really wanted to attend this class. Since it was being offered early in the afternoon on a weekday, doing so meant I would have to request a half day off work. I, of course, felt terrible about asking for personal time off for something that wasn't medically required; still, my bosses continually told me they would support me in any way they could during this time.

I knew it was as important, if not more important, to boost my mental health as it was to care for my physical health. The fact that each person participating in this class would receive a free supply of beauty products made signing up even more irresistible. So, I requested that time away from work, and my boss immediately gave me his blessings.

I was excited for the day, and when the time came, I showed up and joined a group of about six other ladies. Everyone there quickly bonded, and the instructor started demonstrating the proper steps for applying makeup. As I was already familiar with some of the steps taught on best-applying eye makeup, foundation, blush, and lip color, I found myself helping the other students when they had a question, or the instructor was busy helping someone else. Soon, much to my delight, I became the teacher's unofficial aide while being complimented on my beautician skills. They, of course, could have had no idea the hours of practice I had put into this kind of thing over the years. It was such a fun afternoon, and so enjoyable to visit with others who could relate to those things only a fellow cancer patient can feel.

As the class wrapped up, the instructor explained that the cancer society also offered gift certificates to the center's patients for up to $200 to purchase a wig. Those could be picked up from the receptionist's desk of the building we were in at any time. She advised us to buy a wig before we lost our hair since it can be emotionally devastating to a woman to lose yet another form of her identity to cancer.

I didn't know I would lose all my hair when this class took place. It wasn't until after I consulted with my doctor up north that I found out that it would be inevitable. Later, when I was completely bald, I was much more thankful for the knowledge I'd gained that day at the "look good, feel better" class.

My dear friend, Bonnie, offered to go with me whenever I was ready to shop for a wig. I needed to figure out where to shop for one, so I turned to the internet, looking for shops in the Santa Maria area. Once I found the one that looked most promising, I shared that information with her, and we made a date of when we would drive over and shop there. We also made plans to have dinner together after that.

It was a challenge finding the place and even harder finding a place to park. We finally managed to do so and began our little adventure. It was overwhelming when we entered the store as I looked around at all the wigs on the wall. I had no idea where to start.

The store owner suggested I try to find a color and style somewhat similar to my own. She explained that not changing the way I looked too drastically would be one more way for me to feel like I wasn't handing my identity over to my cancer.

The search began. Bonnie and I had a blast. We were both trying on wigs in different styles and colors while laughing and teasing each other's reflections in the mirror. We had the store owner take pictures of us together, both wearing wigs. I finally chose the one I was most comfortable in; the same one Bonnie and the store owner agreed looked best on me. Once the purchase was made, which was just a tiny amount over the value of my certificate, once I added in a nylon cap to go underneath the wig, we thanked the store owner and left.

We walked back to the car laughing and headed out for dinner. We chose a restaurant in the nearby shopping mall and enjoyed a nice meal, a glass of wine, and some girl talk. It was getting close to the time to head north for my first chemo infusion, and once those treatments started, I would not be able to drink alcoholic beverages for a minimum of three months. I was going to reasonably enjoy what I could before that time. At the end of our meal, I pulled my wallet out to pay for my fair share, but Bonnie wouldn't hear of it. "It's on me," she insisted, and once again, I felt the glow of true friendship.

Chapter Five
Out in the Open

At some point in time, my mother, who had been off her meds for a while since she had been doing so well, showed signs of her numbers going up again. Our doctor started her back on her treatments. She, too, would be receiving the weekly chemo shots, and with Dad now gone and unable to drive her, Dave and I did our best to schedule her appointments close to mine, so we could take her. Soon, Dave was leaving work to pick me up from the house and drive around the corner to pick Mom up so he could get us both to the cancer center. Mom and I sat side by side, waiting for our shots.

It did give us all an opportunity to visit, and sometimes we would stop at a restaurant for a bite to eat on the way home. Other times, when we could not get our appointments to coincide, there was a van service provided by the cancer center, and a driver would come right to the house to pick Mom up and bring her home after that.

After some time on her treatment, she started having the itching reaction she had experienced in the past, and it became unbearable for her. Our doctor recommended an alternate remedy, an immuno-therapy infusion that would require her to be hooked up to an IV for four to five hours. She was not happy at the prospect of sitting for that long for treatment. After all, think of all the things she could be doing instead. She and I were driving somewhere one day when she expressed her dismay at having to sacrifice a full day out of her busy schedule to sit and have treatment. I looked at her and said, "Mother, I am going to have to spend a month in the hospital soon for a stem cell transplant; how do you think I feel?" She didn't say another word.

So, an appointment was scheduled for Mom to undergo her first infusion. Due to the possibility of her having an initial adverse reaction to the drug, it was explained that patients often have to break down their 1st treatment into two sessions over two days. This allows the drug to be administered into the body at a much slower rate, lessening the chance of a bad reaction. On the day of her first treatment, she got a ride from the transportation service provided by the cancer center.

While at work that day, I got a call from Jeanette, telling me that our mother had had a terrible reaction to the treatment and was taken by ambulance from the cancer center to the hospital right next door. She had to stay the night there.

My sister explained Mom had called her at work while she was hooked up to the IV, saying she felt like she was going to die. This medication can cause a reaction in the lungs that makes you feel like you can't breathe or that you are drowning. This was the case with our mother, leading her to have a panic attack.

Jeanette worked in Santa Maria at the time and left work abruptly to go be by her side. Mom was released from the hospital early the following morning and came home.

Mom also had other health issues going on. There were concerns with her heart, and Jeanette's husband, Corky, had dedicated much of his time to taking her to doctor appointments in Santa Barbara, a city fifty miles south of us. Various tests were run, and we waited anxiously for answers and for her insurance provider to authorize more tests.

Mom sat in my living room one evening not long after we lost Dad and choked up as she expressed concern that she probably only had about another year left to live.

"Mom," I cried, "why would you say that?"

With cancer, the continuing fatigue, and now the concerns with her heart, she felt that she would soon be on her way out. I, of course, did what I could to soothe her concerns. She was 83, and while we knew she had slowed down, she was still full of life and energy. Mom didn't want to miss a thing and often ignored our pleas to stay home rather than attend her many social events.

In early February 2018, management offered me the position of collections supervisor. I was over the moon. After thirty years of employment with the company, years and years of college, homework, sacrifices, struggles, and a yearlong management course behind me, I finally felt some progression. There, of course, was the concern looming in my mind that I would soon need to be out of work for a month. I reminded my boss of this when he made this offer. He looked at me and said, "We will proceed as we would if that were not a factor."

After accepting their offer, the management team gathered all the employees in the department for a quick meeting to announce my promotion. I proudly told them all what an honor it was to be their supervisor and that their dreams to excel were my dreams to help them fulfill. I envisioned mentoring those who wanted to progress, with encouragement and leadership, along with the tools they needed to succeed. How satisfying it would feel to be a part of their accomplishments.

The president of our department sent out an all-employee announcement via email regarding my new role, inviting others to join the collections department in congratulating me. Many congratulatory emails hit my inbox immediately, and I responded with thanks and a message of sincere excitement. I was so flattered by all of it. I couldn't wait to tell my family.

There was a daydream I had had for quite a while of walking into my parents' house, dressed in my work attire, and carrying on a conversation with the two of them at their kitchen counter while waiting to see if they noticed the title on my name tag had changed from collections officer to either collections supervisor or collections manager.

Unfortunately, Dad did not live to see this. This scenario didn't even play out as planned with my mother, as I could not resist calling my family members with my joyous news as soon as I got home from work that day. They were, of course, happy for me. Still, they didn't say it, but I knew they were also concerned about me taking a position with more authority due to my sensitive persona. When I told my mother, her first reaction was sincere excitement. Then, she hesitated and asked, "Aren't you scared?"

"Yes," I answered, "I'm terrified." Deep down inside, I was afraid to be in an authoritative position. Still, my desire to progress and be part of the management team had a hold on me I simply couldn't shake.

Though I cannot recall the precise time frame, it was shortly after that my cell phone rang while I was at work and getting ready to leave my desk for lunch. As usual, my initial reaction to my phone going off in the middle of the workday was frustration. I hated getting personal calls at work. My mood quickly softened when I heard the familiar voice of the lead nurse from the infusion room of the cancer center where I received treatments. As I walked out of the office, we started talking, and she told me the time for the edition of the *Day of Hope* newspaper, which comes out every April here, was fast approaching. This is an annual fundraiser in our area where volunteers hit the street to sell notable edition newspapers to raise money for various cancer-related causes.

Ironically enough, I had been one of those volunteers a couple of times in years past. The financial institution I worked for was one of the local businesses that supported this cause by selling these papers, and I volunteered to be a part of it. In fact, my doctor had been a guest in the group of people sponsoring the drive during one of those times. This was before I was diagnosed and became his patient, but after my mother had become his patient. He and his team had gathered in front of our building for pictures with our CEO and staff members that had volunteered to sell papers. I approached this doctor and re-introduced myself to him, asking if he remembered me from when we met at Roger's bedside and when I took my mother in for her appointments. He thought he did.

The nurse said they were gathering stories to go into this year's edition, and my name came up as a potential candidate to be amongst those patients who might want to contribute their stories for the paper. Would I be interested in being a part of it? She asked. My first thought, of course, was, "Oh, hell no." Then I thought, "Wait … this would be a great way to make my situation known by making it public, and then I would not have to tell it over and over to numerous people. How convenient it would be to have this out in the open at the same time frame I was looking at having to be out of work on disability." The transplant process was expected to start sometime in April, when the papers were published and circulated.

So, I agreed. The nurse explained that someone from the paper would call me to do a phone interview, so we set up a time on the weekend for them to contact me. She did say I would have to agree to have my picture taken, as it was required to be part of the article. I told her that would be fine. The thought of coming clean with my diagnosis after months of silence was a welcome relief, as was the idea that someone else would spare me having to tell it multiple times myself.

The call with the newspaper reporter was scheduled for a Sunday morning shortly after that, and on that day, I sat cuddled up on the couch with my cup of coffee and chatted with a young lady from the paper. I had been thinking that maybe the fact that my mother and I were both battling together against the same type of cancer would make for a great story. The vision of a headline that read "Mother and daughter fight together" against the same form of cancer, along with a picture showing us sitting side by side at the clinic, simultaneously getting our shots, kept running through my mind.

Mom would have loved it. I brought up the situation in our conversation, thinking the reporter might find this coincidence interesting enough to talk about, but she didn't bite. So, I left it alone.

We had a pleasant conversation that went well beyond the scope of my situation. When we were done, the reporter let me know that a photographer from the newspaper would be in touch with me to set up a time for him to take photos and said she would provide him my phone number. I asked Dave if he would like to be in the picture with me and suggested we have our dog in it, too. Since I talk about taking long walks with our dog, Smokey, in the story, I thought it would be fitting. He agreed, and we tried to decide where best to take it. In front of the house or out by the trails where I often walked with Smokey? We decided it would be nice to have it taken next to the water fountain in our front yard.

It is now March, and getting close to the time I would need to consult with the doctors up north to discuss my stem cell transplant. Again, April was the anticipated time frame for the procedure, and through my oncologist, we were scheduled to see the doctor handling my case. The hospital I would be going to is approximately two hundred miles from where we live. It is not a trip you want to make up and back in one day.

Dave's sister, Michele, lives in Watsonville, about an hour from the facility, so we drove up the night before, stayed with her, and drove to my appointment in the morning.

When we got there, I went to the ladies' room and left Dave sitting in the lobby. In my absence, a gentleman approached Dave and asked him what he was being treated for. Dave explained it was not him but his wife who had cancer, and he told him about our situation.

This person told Dave that he had been a patient there for some time and had undergone a procedure similar to what I would be having. He assured us that we were at the best facility for this kind of thing and in the best possible hands. Having someone who could share his experience firsthand was comforting. That is, until he explained that the impression we were under concerning the thirty days I would stay in the hospital for transplant and go home after that was not how this worked.

Wait … what??

He told us that the stem cell transplant was an outpatient process and that I would have to come there a couple of times for a couple of different procedures before it took place. On top of us having to stay in the area for a specific time frame for these additional appointments, he said the mandatory thirty-day stay started after the transplant was complete. He said the hospital often worked with local hotels to help arrange patients' needs at a discounted rate.

Dave and I were both baffled. Both my oncologists had explained that this would be an inpatient procedure. The thought of spending a solid month in the hospital was daunting enough. Still, the idea of making more trips back and forth with Dave having the burden of being my caretaker between visits was way worse. It was also much more time-consuming, which meant a longer leave of absence from work for me. I was sure this gentleman had it all wrong. We said goodbye to him and found our way to check in for my appointment.

Chapter Six
Treatments for Transplant

We first met with a social worker who gathered some personal information from us and explained the programs some local hotels and apartments offered patients and caretakers to stay at. Our insurance carrier may reimburse some of these costs, and we were anxious to learn all we could. We asked about the month's stay versus the multiple visits we were told about, and this young lady confirmed that the transplant procedure was, in fact, inpatient and that I would be in there for thirty days. *Whew,* Dave and I both breathed a sigh of relief.

It was unfortunately short-lived as when my doctor and her assistant came in shortly after that, they told us that this procedure had been an inpatient procedure in the past, but this was no longer the case. Between the two of them, they explained, just like that gentleman had earlier explained to us, that it would consist of multiple visits back and forth to the facility for treatments leading up to the transplant, along with an appointment to collect my stem cells when the time was right.

We were crushed. This meant a much longer interruption in our lives. First and foremost, in my mind, was the additional time I would be away from my job. I could not return to the office between appointments once the chemotherapy treatments started, since my compromised immune system would be even more fragile.

We also learned that the chemo treatments I would be getting would cause me to lose my hair. No worse news could have been delivered that day, and once again, I felt the wind had been knocked out of me. We were also angry about being given the wrong information about the hospital stay from what we thought was a member of their own staff. Patients should not have to deal with any more stress than what they were already under, and nothing else could have devastated me more at that moment. The doctor's assistant explained that this person was not a hospital staff member but someone who gathered patient information to process paperwork for insurance purposes, housing needs, and eligibility for financial assistance programs. I get it, but it did not soften the blow. After being given this news, I could only think of how much I could use a good, strong drink. We couldn't get out of there fast enough.

Unfortunately, the traffic in that area is chaotic and very heavy, and it would be a couple of hours of stop-and-go driving before we could pull off to a restaurant for a drink and a bite to eat.

Dave and I both ordered cocktails, and while the waitress couldn't have known how badly we needed them and fast, it took forever for her to return with them. So long, in fact, that I wanted to get up and go find the bar and get it myself.

It felt like nothing could go our way that day. We were about the only customers there, and there should have been no reason for such a long delay. The food and the service left a lot to be desired. Still, the drink softened the blow a bit, allowing me to calm my nerves and drain some of my disappointments. The long ride home was a somber one that finished late, and we turned in with the anticipation of preparing ourselves to return to work in the morning.

The following day, my manager asked if my appointment went well. I told him, "No, not really," stressing that I would rather not talk about it then. I wanted to take my usual defense of burying my mind in my work and not thinking about my situation.

The next day was Saturday, and I went over to talk with my mother and updated her on my appointment since I had not spoken with her about it. I shared my disappointment in learning that my stay up north would be more than one-and-done in thirty consecutive days, as had been our impression for the past five months.

She felt my pain and sympathized with me, fully knowing my frustration at the extra added time away and the changes it would bring about. It was especially concerning that I was trying to settle into a new position that added more responsibilities and would demand that I fulfill higher expectations. "What next?" she asked in despair. Unfortunately, we would find that out much sooner than expected.

On Sunday, I made my usual call to her. It was not often that much more than a day or two went by that we didn't talk or see each other. I asked how she was doing, and she said she was totally exhausted. I told her to take it easy and not to push herself. I begged her to forego the Bridge game scheduled for the following day so she could stay home and rest. She would not hear of it. Monday Bridge had been a weekly social event for her for years and years. Mom loved playing Bridge, though she often complained that she had played a lousy game when I inquired about it at the end of the day. To even consider forgoing a game would mean she would be letting her partner down by backing out, and besides, she seemed to always be the one to provide the snacks and finger foods the players looked forward to every Monday, and she didn't want to disappoint. "I can sit and relax at Bridge the same as I can sit and relax here at home," she told me firmly.

"So be it," I thought as I hung up the phone.

Monday morning, I got a call while at work from a close friend of my mother's, who lives up the street from her. She had gotten a call from one of my mother's Bridge club players, who said that Mom had a strange episode during the game. She had suddenly become disorientated and incoherent. Her motor skills and speech were impeded, and concerned players wanted to take her to the emergency room at the nearby hospital. Mom wouldn't hear of it. Too many trips to the ER in the recent past, be it on her behalf or my father's, where countless hours were spent waiting to be seen and few results provided when they were, had taken their toll on her. I completely understood her reluctance.

Her friend explained that one of the Bridge players was driving her home and asked if I could meet them there. She told me Mom had tried to get up and drive herself home, and the players had to prevent her from doing so by taking her car keys away from her. I assured her that I would be there soon.

It was, in fact, already about time for me to go to lunch anyway. In all honesty, I did not feel a sense of urgency at that moment and worked first to wrap up what I had going on at my desk.

Soon, Mom's friend called again and asked when I thought I would be there, as Mom was already home. I told her I was on my way. Since Mom had had a series of doctor appointments and numerous other minor (or so we thought) issues lately, I assumed it to be just another little setback, and she would simply need a quick check-in, where I would console her and be on my way back to the office. Mom's friend was at the house, as was the Bridge player who drove her home. Mom sat on the couch with her back to the kitchen, and when entering the house from the garage, I did not go directly to her but instead spoke first with the two women regarding the situation as we tried to decide the best course of action to take.

Mom was still somewhat incoherent and not convinced that a trip to the ER was what she wanted to do. "What are they going to do for me?" was her plea to dissuade us from taking her. I knew Mom had recently been seen by a new doctor, but I did not know this person's name or phone number since my sister and her husband had been arranging those visits. We three women rummaged through Mom's appointment books and paperwork, trying to get that information so we could call the doctor for advice. In her current state of mind, we couldn't get Mom to answer our questions logically.

Though I can't recall which medical facility I was finally able to reach to talk to medical staff and explain my mother's symptoms, the person on the line advised me to get her to the nearest emergency room immediately so she could be assessed.

After hanging up, I went to where my mother sat on the couch, and for the first time since arriving at the house, I saw her face. Her lips were blue, and her eyes showed a sense of desperate confusion. The shock of seeing her like this caused my heart to stop and pushed me into panic mode. "Come on, Mom," I insisted, "I'm taking you to the ER now."

She reluctantly let us help her off the couch and out to my car. I remember being taken aback when noticing all the cat hair clinging to her clothing. My mother was always meticulous in her appearance, and it wasn't like her to allow such imperfections to go unnoticed. Still, she did have a cat that was somewhat new to the household, so I figured she may not have realized how much shedding it was doing.

With Mom finally seated comfortably in the car, I locked up the house. Her Bridge companion said she would drive and meet us at the hospital. The hospital is about ten or twelve minutes from our homes, and after circling the parking lot several times there, with no luck finding parking close to the door of the ER, we settled for a spot on the street. I tried to get her from the car to the front door of the ER. It was either her Bridge friend or one of the hospital staff who, upon seeing our struggle, asked if we needed a wheelchair.

"Oh, that would be nice."

After sitting Mom down in the car, I ran to the hospital's entrance to grab a wheelchair and went back to help her. The waiting room there was much busier than it usually was for our small town, and I knew there had been a high number of flu cases in our area recently. Many very sick people were waiting to be seen, as well as some victims who had been involved in a car accident that morning. I was concerned about how long it would be before someone could get to her.

As soon as I could speak with the receptionist checking people in, I explained our plight as quickly as possible and then added, "Just so you know, I don't like the color of her lips."

Thankfully, we were called back much quicker than I expected, and medical staff began taking her vitals, asking her questions while hooking her up to monitors. In an attempt to fill in the blanks where Mom couldn't, the gentleman assessing her asked me to explain some of the ways Mom was acting out of the norm. I told him she was unusually quiet, as to where she usually talks a lot. At that moment, Mom looked straight at me with a somewhat wounded look in her eyes and, with what would turn out to be her last words to me, asked, "I do?"

Feeling terrible, I responded, "Mom, I didn't mean it that way, but you're usually very social."

The physician continued his work and was eventually joined by other physicians. I stepped outside the curtain of the examining room when they moved on to perform tasks of a more personal nature, returning to her side to hold her hand again once they were done.

After a while, she seemed to relax and lay quietly; her eyes remained open but vacant. I was thankful she appeared to be resting, though I was concerned she was not responding to my attempts to converse with her. Several times, the left side of her body seemed to convulse as she squeezed my arm as if she was trying to hold onto me. Bending over her, I held her arm and said, "I'm here, Mom; I got you."

I had had the opportunity to text Dave when stepping out of the examining room earlier, letting him know where I was and why. I asked him to meet me at the hospital when he got off work. Mom's Bridge partner had been back to see Mom, and I took a seat in the waiting room while she did so. She came out from the exam room area, in through the waiting room at an anxious pace, and said, "This doesn't look good." She didn't slow her step when she looked me in the eye and said, "You shouldn't be here."

I figured she must be referring to my compromised immune system and my vulnerability to being in an emergency room full of sick people with various illnesses. While I knew Mom would have shared my health situation with some friends and family members, I was not at all sure who she had or had not told up to this point.

Dave arrived, and once he knew exactly what was going on and how serious he felt this was, he called Jeanette, who was at work in Santa Maria, to let her know what was happening. I had an appointment scheduled that evening with the photographer, who would take my picture for the *Day of Hope* newspaper article. I quickly texted him to reschedule for the following evening. That appointment would also end up being canceled. In fact, the photo shoot would end up not taking place at all. I later learned that the paper agreed to publish the article without my picture.

Soon, Jeanette and Brian arrived at the hospital, and Dave and I left, driving our vehicles home so we could come back in one. Dave did not want me going back into the hospital, mask or no mask, and since my siblings were there, I conceded. He and I returned to town to get a bite to eat and drive my mother's car home, as it was still parked at the facility where she had been playing Bridge earlier.

Sometime in the wee hours of the morning, it was determined that our local hospital was not equipped to diagnose or treat our mother; therefore, she was transported by ambulance to the ICU of a hospital in Santa Barbara, a town fifty miles south of us. There, she spent the next couple of days on life support while a team of competent doctors assessed her condition and compared their medical opinions.

They then arranged a meeting between themselves, our family, and the hospital's social worker to discuss her condition and have us decide how we wanted to proceed. As ill as Barbara was with her COPD, she could not make the trip to Santa Barbara, and she was part of the conversation through the speaker on Jeanette's cell phone.

Mom had a multitude of health issues going on. It was determined she had had several small strokes the day she was brought to our local hospital. Her heart was one of the most precarious issues, and the doctors doubted Mom would survive heart surgery should they take that route. They also felt that if she did survive, she would require extensive physical therapy and probably never regain the ability to live the life she had been accustomed to. The doctors asked if she would be happy living a life like that. No. Mother was a socialite, taking great pride in her endless energy and meticulous appearance. Anything short of her ability to continue being that person would have been an insult to her, leaving her with a life not worth her effort.

Mother had been very explicit vocally, and in her written directive that should she ever have to rely on life support, we were to take her off immediately. Period.

I really tried to hold it together during that meeting, but there came the point where I couldn't help but fall apart. How could this be happening just ten months after losing Dad? How could we possibly have to make such a daunting decision when we were not prepared for this? The hard truth was, it was not our decision to make. Mom had already made it for us, and we had no right to go against her wishes. Still, it would be another night and another day of discussion between the extended family members before we were willing to come to terms with it and let the doctors know.

I remember standing in my mask at the nurse's station the evening this inevitable decision hung in our midst as we conversed with the nurse on duty. She looked at me, tears soaking the material of my mask under my eyes, my nose running and soaking it through to my mouth, while I dabbed at my face with a tissue. What a sight I must have been.

"Aww," she moaned, looking at me as if she wanted to hold me in her arms and hug me. I would have welcomed it had she offered.

Chapter Seven
The Song of Our Nest

Mom passed the following day, March 15th, 2018, ten months to the day after our father had. Services would be held on March 26th, 2018, ten months to the day after services had been held for him. She was laid to rest next to him. The services happened to fall on a Monday, fitting for the gathering of so many of her friends that usually gathered with her on Mondays for Bridge.

Many people shared stories of our mother with those in attendance. She truly was loved by many. I had gathered the courage that day, at the end of her eulogy, to recite a poem I had written to her many years before called "The Song of our Nest." I hadn't planned for this and didn't have it with me, so I had to do my best to recite it from memory. After reviewing that poem, which I had not read in a long time, I would later realize that I'd left out a couple of verses. I will always be glad, though, that I shared it there. I knew there wouldn't be another opportunity to do so. I will also never forget the pride I felt after leaving the podium once I recited it, returning to the seat beside my husband and son, and hearing Dave whisper, "Honey, that was awesome."

Several people took a moment at the reception to compliment me on my reading, some asking for a copy of my poem. We were all so thankful for the outpouring of love from family and friends that day; Mom would have been proud of the turnout.

"The Song of Our Nest"

I awoke this morning to a song playing softly in my heart,
I could feel in my soul the strumming of notes on a harp.

The notes, they grew louder, and an orchestra joined in,
A little bird perched upon my window to sing her solo again.

She sang to me of days past, all surrounded by love,
And told me of five children sewn to fit like a glove.

They began their young lives with parents who each gave,
Not just to one but to all, a single path in which to pave.

Each and every one in this circle gladly stood,
Beside one another, be it bad times or good.

So began a pact, their dedication so strong,
No outside force could break through this sacred song.

And as they grew older to see our Lord's way,
He blessed all with hope for new glory each day.

On lived this family, though tragedy was dealt,
In which all to experience, the loss of one felt.

Still held together while all shattered in soul,
To hold each other's love in their palm was their goal.

But even while the hole in this circle still mended,
Again came those troubles fate seems to like lending.

Tight pulled the rope of this circle around,
All the wisdom in which the threads built had been wound.

So kept the pact of this love burning so bright,
That no mountain known to man has arisen its height.

If you listen to the message these lines try to give,
I feel you must recognize the nest where we've all lived.

And while the young birds of this nest have lifted their wings,
We all fly with the power to make one another sing.

So now, to you, I give thanks from the depths of my heart,
For making my life encircled with love from the start.

Sandra R. Pickles

November 11, 1983

Having some family members in town for a couple of days during this time was helpful. As is typically the case, though, those people go home and move on, and we try to accept the new void in our lives and do our best to try to learn to live with it.

While this was difficult for me as a daughter, friend, and neighbor, it was especially hard for Brian. Not only had he been spending a good majority of time at home with Mom in the months leading up to her passing, but he had also depended on her for emotional support for years with his health issues. With Dad and Mom both gone now, we were very concerned about how he would hold up.

I took the day after the services off from work and stayed home alone in what I called a "me day." This was in an effort to unwind and clear my head before entering into my usual line of defense from the world: work! Drowning myself in the office setting and trying to adjust to the supervisor role was my goal as I returned to the office and tried to begin the healing process.

Other issues were weighing heavy on my mind as well since we were closing in on the end of March, which meant we would soon be into April. The story of my own health issues would be coming out in the paper that month, not to mention April would be the beginning of my appointments up north to prepare for my transplant. I would start my disability leave from work soon, and again, except for my managers and one coworker, no one in my department knew yet of my situation.

This special edition newspaper was set to come out Thursday, April 12th, and my last day at work before my disability was set to begin would be Friday, April 13th. A weekly staff meeting was held every Wednesday in our department, and since my story would be in the paper the following morning, I felt this would be the perfect time to make an announcement to my coworkers. I let my manager know that I would like to take a minute after the meeting to give the team a heads-up that I would be out of the office for a while.

He agreed. Once he had finished up with the order of business that morning, I went to the front of the group and let them know I needed to share something with them. Before making my way to the front of the group, one of my coworkers asked if this was good news.

"Well, not for me, it isn't," I said. So, though I was accustomed to speaking in front of my coworkers and thought I would be okay with doing it now, I found myself stumbling over my words. The heat rose in my face as I told them; it turned out that I had some serious health issues that needed to be addressed that would require me to be out of the office for an undetermined amount of time. I let them know there would be an article in the paper the following day if they had questions, and I left it at that. The team respected the fact that I didn't want to elaborate, and the workday continued as usual.

The following morning, the paper came out. Since our financial institution has many employees who volunteered to sell this special edition at various locations, I assume the story was read by some of them right away.

I hoped the news would spread quickly. Having worked there for thirty years, most employees had dealt with me, if not in person, at least on the phone, and we all had a good rapport. When I appeared at work Thursday morning, it was apparent my coworkers knew of my situation and diagnosis. They were in a group talking in low voices when I entered, and they quietly gathered around my desk to offer sympathy and support. One of my coworkers, who had worked with me for the past couple of years, and whom I had mentored when she joined the department, had tears in her eyes as I approached the group. As I came and stood in front of her, looking her in the eyes, I hugged her as her tears broke, and she cried in my arms.

Trying to soothe her, I said, "I am going to be okay. I'm going to go 'Sandra' on it." This was an expression used amongst us in the department, which meant that someone had pushed me to the point of losing my temper, and I, for lack of a better term, "went off" on them. It didn't happen often, but once in a while, it was inevitable in our line of work. I hoped she would understand how determined I was to fight this disease by using this expression.

After we dried her tears, we took time as a group for me to open up about everything I had been going through. I answered their questions, telling them, to the best of my knowledge, what I would be looking at regarding treatment. They were all so shocked at every-thing they were just learning and were so generous in offering to help in any way. We were a tight-knit group, and it was common for us to do nice things for one another if one of us was in need. They were so anxious to lend a hand. A few of them discussed starting a GoFundMe page for Dave and me in anticipation of doctor bills, travel expenses, hotel rooms, and lost hours at work. I let them know that while we appreciated it, and a family member had already suggested it, we would prefer not to. Somehow, we would work it all out … right!?

With just two workdays looming before my departure, I tried to wrap up as much as possible of my work projects. Much to my surprise, our acting CEO called an all-branch staff meeting in our board room that afternoon, with just a half-hour warning to employees, to present me with a check from the management team to help Dave and me with upcoming expenses. After he gave a short speech and gave me an encouraging hug, other employees took the time to wish me well and offer support in any way they could. Everyone was so generous in their offers to do my grocery shopping, clean my house, mow our lawn, or do anything else I needed. One coworker said, "This must kind of make you feel like a celebrity."

"Yes," I told him, "it kind of does."

He offered to come over and walk my dog while I was gone if I needed.

Unbeknownst to me, employees in my department and those in the department where I had done my management training were planning a potluck for me the following day. This was organized by the young lady who had cried in my arms, and she had stayed up till the wee hours of that Friday morning making up burgundy t-shirts for employees to wear that day with the logo #Team Sandra. I learned that burgundy is the color that represents myeloma cancer. My shirt was black in order to stand out as the honoree. The food was great, and everyone made a point to show me how much they cared. A photoshoot was taken with the branch staff and me in front of the building and posted to our company's Facebook page. Our public relations officer taking the pictures remarked that I really took everyone by surprise with this news. I told him I hadn't wanted to make a fuss.

Throughout that day, much of my time was spent in my manager's office as he and I tried to prepare for my departure. Out of his office window, I saw numerous employees dropping by my desk, hoping to say goodbye. I missed most of them by being in his office behind closed doors, but I waved and smiled at them through the window if I could. Once back at my desk, one employee that had worked there for years came and hugged me, asking, "Why didn't you tell us?"

I told her I hadn't wanted to make a fuss, that I wanted to spread sunshine, not sadness. I assured her that this would all be done and over soon, and we would be back having a glass of wine together at the local club before she knew it.

I opened one of the cards that had been left at my desk and inside found a beautiful pewter trinket with what looked like an angel or a fairy godmother sitting on a stage, pink laced curtains drawn behind her. Above the curtains, it read, "Always have faith. Always believe." I read the card, learning that it was from one of the employees in the department I had mentored in and with whom I had sat next to. We had become very close in the months I was there, and the emotions that hit me at that moment were overwhelming. I held back tears as I walked over to her desk to hug and thank her. I told my friend I was naming this fairy godmother "Tinkerbell" and promised I would keep her by my side during my treatments, and I did.

Before the day was through, I was able to say goodbye to several employees in different departments and was again touched by the hugs and support received from so many. At 5 p.m., after leaving an out-of-office message response on my email, I turned my computer off and said goodbye for what I thought would be six to eight weeks.

Chapter Eight
Chemotherapy

Dave and I were scheduled for a consultation class with the hospital staff up north early Tuesday morning to review my upcoming procedure and sign consent forms. This would be a group course with other patients with multiple myeloma who would also be undergoing a stem cell transplant. It was said we must be on time, as the class would not stop its progress for latecomers once it started. We drove down the night before and took our place at the table in plenty of time before class started.

I had chosen to begin my leave of absence from work on Monday, April 16th, 2018. I spent that day packing for the five nights we would be gone, quietly reflecting on those events which had already taken place and those that were soon to come.

That past Friday, I told my coworkers in one of our conversations that I was trying to look at this as an adventure. One I wasn't looking forward to but was looking forward to getting started, so I could be done with it. I was so naïve in thinking that once the transplant was over, my body, my brain, and my life would soon return to normal—another one of those instances, I guess, where ignorance is bliss.

Dave went ahead to work a full day on Monday, and we hit the road as soon as he was home and packed. We were into the drive an hour or so when a call came through on Dave's cell phone. I answered it since he was driving. It was the young lady from his health insurance carrier who had been overseeing our case. She told me my stem cell transplant had just been approved.

"I'm sure glad to hear that," I said, "since we're on our way now to start the process." We had been through so many medical procedures preparing for this that had been covered by insurance already that we assumed it had already been authorized. Still, good to know.

We guesstimated our arrival time to the hotel to be around 10 p.m., figuring in a stop for dinner. However, upon approaching the town of Soledad, the friendly voice on our GPS warned us of slow traffic twenty miles ahead. That casual warning turned into two hours of standstill traffic, which we heard may have been caused by an accident involving an overturned truck. We sat for what seemed like forever.

Many people turned their cars off and got out to talk with other drivers as they consulted their cell phones to find out the cause of the delay. When we finally moved on, we saw no evidence of a wreck. Two hours plus must have been more than sufficient time to clear the road of any evidence. What we did see sitting in one of the lanes on the highway, in the path of the now-moving traffic, was a big black vehicle that appeared to have been abandoned during the delay. I wondered if the driver had run out of gas and left to get help. My biggest concern was the potential of an accident being caused by someone coming up fast behind this black vehicle blocking their path in the dark of night. We trusted that law enforcement had been monitoring this situation and was aware it was there and that it would be taken care of.

We finally arrived at our hotel around or after midnight. It turned out to be an area a little less desirable than we expected. Confirming our impression were the low voices that drifted our way, along with a scent that smelled suspiciously of marijuana, coming from around the corners of the building as we circled around the front of the hotel. Dave chose to keep our truck parked overnight in the area designated and limited for visitor registration, since it was an area lit and visible from our room. This was in hopes that it would be there and be intact come morning.

Class began at 8:45, and we took our places around a table with a group of staff and approximately ten other people made up of patients and their caregivers. As I later discovered, this process would not be humanly possible to go through alone, especially after the transplant.

Soon after class started, we were interrupted by a couple being escorted into the room by a staff member. They had been delayed either by traffic, car trouble, or maybe trouble parking. The hospital and the surrounding area had been undergoing major construction for some time. Maneuvering through traffic and construction detours to find parking in the designated area, making your way to the parking lot elevator, and to the bus stop to wait for the shuttle bus to transport you to the front of the hospital is an endeavor in and of itself. I could certainly understand getting delayed.

Class resumed, and one of the class coordinators sat to the side with this couple and brought them up to speed on what we'd already covered. We were briefed on what we could expect through our scheduled procedures, and then we signed those consent forms required by the hospital for them and their doctors to proceed without liability. The meeting lasted a couple of hours.

There was one patient in the group who appeared to have difficulty breathing. I believe he is older than me, though I can't really guess by how much. I can't help but worry about how he will get through all this. I said a silent prayer for him and hoped he'd be okay.

Another class was scheduled for the group to attend shortly after this one, which covered various aspects of the transplant procedure and its before and aftercare. This took place in a large room, where a gentleman stood behind a podium at the right front and presented a slideshow on a projector located to our left in the darkened room. We weren't able to sit as close to the front as I would have liked to. I am one who always wants to take the first or second row in a class, a habit that came about from hoping to gain an advantage throughout the many college classes I had taken. In my mind, being able to hear clearly is first and foremost in being successful in any learning environment. We were somewhere in the middle of the room, and adding to my frustration was the fact that someone behind us was talking. I complained to Dave about how rude this person was.

I would later feel terrible upon learning that the person talking was an interpreter for one of the patients.

There was also someone in the audience breathing and wheezing so heavily that it too impaired our ability to hear clearly. It turned out to be the gentleman from our first class that I had been concerned about earlier.

Again, I felt guilty for my impatience in situations that couldn't be helped. Doing our best to follow along, I strained to catch every word and take notes.

Soon, we hear the distinct sound of a fire alarm. Our presenter tells us not to worry about it and continues doing what he is doing. As the alarm continues, we participants eventually become restless.

The door to the room we occupied had a little pane of glass in it so that those entering could see those exiting and vice versa. We could see and hear staff outside talking and moving about the area in response to the warning. The alarm was not slowing or stopping as our presenter had indicated it would. He continued to try to convince us that everything was fine.

I guess he took his teaching role very seriously and was determined to complete the task he set out to do. As more minutes passed, we could hear the voices of those outside the room grow louder, with strained overtones.

Footsteps moved faster and heavier in intensity, and we students in the room grew restless and concerned, shuffling about in our seats, whispering amongst each other. Finally, a gentleman entered the room and told our teacher we needed to clear the space and evacuate the building, like, *now.*

Something all of us students were more than ready and willing to do. We got up quickly and left the room, closely following staff's instructions to go out and gather outside the hospital's main entrance. There was already a large group of people waiting there. Some patients were in wheelchairs. The person who had been presenting our class was standing near us, and Dave asked him if this happened often.

"Never in all the time I've worked here have we ever had a fire alarm," he answered, and he had been there for many years. We could hear the sirens of the approaching firetrucks confirming that this was no drill. Two or three trucks pulled to the front area, and fire personnel entered the building. After some time, they came out, gave the all-clear signal, then loaded back up in their trucks and left.

The crowd dispersed, many re-entering the building. Dave and I returned to resume and complete our class, though many students did not return. We'd had a full day, and I'm guessing we ended it by grabbing a bite to eat and heading back to our hotel. As I write this, it is close to three years since these events occurred, and many details have faded from my memory.

The following morning, we were back at the hospital, so I could have bloodwork done and get a chest X-ray. I was scheduled to see my doctor and get an EKG that afternoon, and as is often the case, appointments don't start as expected, and we spent a lot of time sitting in waiting rooms.

I was scheduled for surgery at 10:30 the following morning. This was for placing a port, which would be embedded in my chest, to allow medications and other fluids to be administered throughout my body. My doctor had given me an antibacterial scrub during my appointment the day before, instructing me to shower with it that night and the following morning. That was easy enough, but I could not eat or drink anything after midnight on Wednesday, and I truly missed my coffee.

A couple of the gals from the training class we had attended on Tuesday had been scheduled for their surgery much earlier that morning, and Dave and I ran into them in the waiting room. They were already done and assured me the surgery was no big deal. "Piece of cake," they said.

Soon I was prepped in a hospital gown, a hairnet, and on a gurney, being rolled into a room to meet the team of surgeons performing the surgery.

Those who work in the healthcare industry are some of the kindest and most caring people in the world. This group was no exception, and they greeted me with much enthusiasm. Some were laughing, telling me they'd been discussing how much they loved my last name, "Pickles," and wishing their names were as unique. I have gotten, and continually get, many giggles and positive comments regarding the name I took in marriage, and I got a kick out of their teasing. Though my husband will tell you, it wasn't an easy name to grow up with, as he was teased about it as a kid. Our son had also complained of being picked on about our last name when he was a youngster, and I told him it was the name of a family well respected in our community and he should always be proud of it.

I can't say the surgery was as easy as the others seemed to think it was, but once it was done, I had a port in the upper right-hand side of my chest which would remain a part of me until early June.

That same day, I would spend three hours hooked up to an IV to start the circulation of fluids through my body. This was in preparation for administering a chemotherapy drug I would receive the following day. Since I am not a person who is accustomed to sitting for long stretches, I took to my passion for reading. I encouraged Dave to find something to do. At the same time, I perched in my seat next to a window where I could sink comfortably into a story without distraction. After three hours, I was hooked up to a small battery-operated device that would control the circulation of the fluids in the lines hooked to the port in my chest. The device was housed in a protected case that zips up like a suitcase and is placed on a carrier with a handle to hold it or pull it along behind you.

Staff providing the device gave us instructions on its operation and care. Thank God Dave is mechanically inclined because I am not.

The device also has a plug-in option, which we were instructed to use overnight for backup just in case the battery should fail. We returned to the hotel with our tidy little package, which we immediately christened "My Buddy." After all, I would be pulling it along with me for the next couple of days, and we needed to get along. Since I'm always in a hurry to get to where ever it is I am going or do what it is I am doing, I wanted to keep forgetting to grab it when I moved about. For instance, when I was getting in and out of the truck, going to the bathroom, or walking across the room. Thank goodness Dave has a more patient eye for detail and would grab and remind me of it every time I went to move.

This unit had a continuous hum as it performed its duties. Different colors would flash throughout it as it pumped the fluids about. The first night we had it, I woke in a panic, somehow under the impression that the device had stopped working. The quiet, swishing hum this little unit had as it pumped fluid through its little hoses made me feel as if I were sleeping side by side with my heartbeat, and now I could no longer identify that hum. Shaking Dave from his sleep in my panic, he quickly checked it and assured me it was working fine. Maybe I couldn't hear it as well as I thought I should have or misinterpreted the sequence in which the colors were flashing. Knowing that Dave would have recognized if there was a reason to be concerned, and he wasn't, I was able to drift back off to sleep.

In the morning, I woke up and headed to the bathroom. Along the way, I caught the reflection of someone I didn't recognize in the mirror. I stopped dead in my tracks. Wait … it was me. My face and body were so swollen and bloated from all the fluids pumped into me I hadn't recognized the person walking past the mirror.

The appointment for my first chemo infusion was scheduled for 8 a.m. that day. We were up extra early as we knew there was heavy traffic in the city by now, and getting to the hospital would be time-consuming and challenging. We were still learning the best routes to get there from the hotel. For some reason, probably because I was in such a hurry to get this started since it meant I would be done that much sooner, and on my way back to work, I was in high spirits on our way to the hospital. I was reaching out by text to people, particularly my boss, telling them they better watch out when all this was done and over with, as I was coming back full force.

When Dave and I got in the elevator on the hospital's ground floor and pushed the button for the level we needed to head to, he looked at me and asked, "Are you scared?"

I looked him in the eye and said, "No," and I meant it.

The infusion areas were already busy, and I was lucky they had a room to offer me that is used only if other sites are full. It provided me privacy behind closed doors. I even got a bed so I could lie down and have the option of having the lights on or off during the infusion, which would again last several hours. At first, I choose to leave them on, anxiously anticipating picking up where I left off with my book. After convincing Dave to go relax in one of the hospital cafeterias, I started reading.

Soon after that, though, maybe because I was lying down, fatigue overcame me, and I asked for the lights to be turned off so I could sleep. Dave returned to sit with me long before the process was completed.

Once I was done and the nurses wrapped things up, we left and headed toward our hotel. We enjoyed taking in the sites around the area and driving through the business district, which is busy and has many stores we don't have where we live. I love checking out new places.

This would be our last night staying here for this particular trip. I was scheduled to return to the hospital early the following morning, which was Saturday, for bloodwork and to be disconnected from the device (My Buddy) that continued to regulate the flow of fluids in my body. On this day, my face and body were even more bloated, and I was thankful I had brought my fat jeans (come on, ladies, most of us own a pair or two).

Considering my chemotherapy, I felt fine for the rest of that day and the next. Dave was amazed by this, saying, "I can't believe you just had all those drugs pumped into your body, and it doesn't seem to have affected you at all."

I looked at him and said, "Neither can I, but I'm good."

Chapter Nine
The Horrendous Headache

We were eager to get to the hospital and get things done so we could be on our way home. Since this was Saturday, they did not schedule regular appointments on the weekends, and the parking lot, which was usually packed, was almost empty. Not having to use the parking garage or shuttle bus and being able to park right across the way from the front doors of the hospital was great. We headed in to take care of business.

As I would need daily doses in the days ahead of a drug called Neupogen, which is a bone marrow growth factor, Dave needed to be shown how to administer the medication. It had to be kept cold, and I would require two shots in my stomach each morning. After unhooking my IV bag, the staff provided us with the liquid vials of Neupogen. They also gave Dave a crash course in delivering the shots. Something he wasn't overly comfortable with or excited about doing, and I can't say as I blamed him. I certainly wouldn't have wanted to be responsible for administering shots into someone's stomach. Especially my spouse's.

Since we would be on the road for hours after things were done, and this medication needed to be kept cold, we left the hospital and stopped at the Walgreens in town, where we had been filling all my prescriptions. Here we bought a small portable ice chest to put the medication in for the drive home, and we hit the road.

The feeling that I'd just gotten through the first important part of preparing for my stem cell transplant, and done so with flying colors, suddenly put me in the mood for some kick-ass music. I popped one of Dave's and my favorite CDs into the disc player. Immediately, my shoulders were shaking, and my fingers were snapping to the beat of the music as I did my best to dance in the passenger seat. Every song lifted me higher, helping me to feel a little like my old self. Thanks, Bruno. Music is the best medicine!

I will spare you the details of the effects a hefty dose of chemotherapy can do on your digestive system as it courses through your body, other than to say there were a few public restrooms along the way home that day that were violated, as I did my best to sneak in and out of them unnoticed, hoping no one would know who the culprit was responsible for the condition they were left in.

It felt so good to get back home and sleep in our own bed. That was until I woke up the next morning. I felt like I had been hit by a Mack truck. This felt like the world's worst hangover, and I've had some doozies. A delayed reaction to the chemo infusion, I'm sure. You can't imagine what a relief it was to be able to spend the time I needed in bed, which is where I lay for hours.

Dave would return to work the next morning, and I would begin my time at home alone with the days. He would give me my shots early. I pretended they didn't hurt, so he wouldn't feel bad. Since I couldn't get my port or its incision site wet, Dave would tape a plastic bag over the area before he left so I could shower later. I didn't have an appetite, much energy, or any desire to drink the water and other fluids recommended to me to help clear the chemo from my system.

I didn't even have a desire for my morning coffee, as it seemed too heavy on my stomach. I took to drinking a light cup of hot tea with honey in it.

I was required to report to my local oncologist's office on Thursday of that week to change the dressing on my port. This would need to be done weekly now. I also had to have daily blood draws to monitor the bone marrow growth factor level in my blood. Dave drove me to my oncologist's office in Santa Maria every morning to do this, and my lab results had to be faxed to the hospital up north every day by noon.

The growth factor had to reach a certain level before I could go back for the next step in the transplant process, which was apheresis. This is a process where my blood plasma would be withdrawn from my body through a tube hooked up to the port in my chest, separated into plasma and cells where the cells would later be reintroduced into my body. Aka, stem cell transplant. There was no way to pinpoint when my blood levels would reach the point necessary to start the apheresis procedure. Still, once they did, we would need to be ready to return to the hospital immediately to get started. There was a possible start time of May 2nd, penciled in on the hospital's calendar for me to return there. That was unless I was called in earlier.

On that Saturday, following the start of my daily labs, I made the unwise decision to pay a visit to the office where I worked, as some of the collection staff work on Saturdays, and I wanted to say hi. I just hated being away from the job and everyone I worked with.

The visit filled a void I had felt for the past two weeks. While catching up with everyone, one of our upper managers, who happened to be in the building, came by our area and saw me there. Considering my recent treatment, he was concerned about my exposure to other people. He said, "Masks do not protect you the way you think they might." He told us of a friend who had had a double lung transplant and thought he was protected while wearing a mask, but was met with severe consequences. He encouraged me to leave and said, "That's an order."

I was flattered by his genuine concern and followed his orders, returning home immediately. I gave little thought to his story. All my life, I'd been accustomed to being one who didn't get sick much, hardly ever catching what was going around when others did. As I said earlier, it usually only lasted a day or so if I ever had an ache or sniffle. Those days were gone, though. That was back in what I now refer to as BC (before cancer). My immune system was not, and never will be, what it was before. It was so hard to change my mentality from never being concerned about my health to now needing to be overly worried about it. After all, I was fifty-seven, and old habits die hard.

Early to midafternoon the following day, I laid down for a nap. Here again, something I had never done before that was now becoming a common occurrence. The hardest thing was admitting I was so mentally or physically exhausted that I had no choice but to lie down and sleep. Once I accepted that my body was trying to heal itself, rest was easier to surrender to, though I still struggle with it sometimes. I was, and still am, so grateful for the quiet, dim, calming environment of my bedroom, where I can take refuge on a soft pillow, under a cozy blanket, on a comfortable bed. I wish this comfort for anyone suffering from any type of illness.

After napping for a couple of hours, I got up and fixed myself a big bowl of hot cereal and toast. Cream of Wheat and vanilla ice cream sandwiches would soon become the only foods that appealed to me. I'm guessing because they were both light on the stomach and, in their own way, comfort foods. One hot, one cold. For some reason, the nap and meal did not revive me in their usual way, and I begrudgingly returned to my spot under my blanket for a bit more rest.

Dave became concerned early evening when he found me still there and still groggy. When he asked if I was okay, and I tried to blow it off, saying I was fine, he wasn't having it. He grabbed a thermometer that works through an app you plug into your phone (what will they think of next?) and took my temperature several times. The rule we had been given was to call my doctor if my temperature reached 100.4 or higher. I was not quite there, giving me somewhat of a defense in trying to convince Dave I was okay. Again, I don't like to complain or cause a fuss. He still wasn't buying it, though, especially since, on top of the higher-than-normal temperature, I was lethargic and sinking further still.

Mind you, it is Sunday evening, and my doctors are unavailable. Dave starts going through the notebook the hospital had provided us with, which gives pertinent contact information. He finally spoke with someone and explained the situation, asking how concerned he should be and if he should be taking me to the hospital. The person Dave is talking to advises him to take me to the nearest emergency room immediately. Dave ignores my continued protests and tells me to get ready, because he is taking me there now. As I mentioned, the local hospital is a very short distance from us, and we were there in about ten minutes. By this time, I was completely drained of energy and had a hellacious headache.

As soon as we got to the ER, and Dave explained the situation and my condition to the woman handling the front desk, we were escorted through the waiting room and onto the hospital floor. Here they sat me down, took my vitals, put me on a gurney, and hooked me up to a machine. Shortly after being wheeled into a room, a doctor came in to assess me. I recognized her as one of the doctors who worked on my mother when I brought her in less than two months before. Her moves were quick and competent; she hit the hand sanitizer dispensary perched on the wall after each and every time she touched me. All I could think of was the pain in my head, and I kept asking for something to alleviate it. Since they wanted to run blood tests on me, the doctor asked if I had a port, and we said, "Yes."

She did a little happy dance exclaiming, "Oh goody, goody gumdrops." Even in my delirious and painful state of mind, I appreciated her attempt at cheerful humor in this serious situation. My blood was drawn and sent to the lab.

Since it would be a while before results would be available, and based on my condition, it was recommended that I be transferred to the hospital in Santa Maria, where my oncologist worked, so he could access me in the morning and oversee my care. It was required that I be transported by ambulance, and we, of course, wished we had made the drive to Santa Maria to begin with. In any case that you consider an emergency, though, you naturally gravitate to the nearest hospital. The nearest ER had been the order given by the person Dave spoke with on the phone.

By this time, it was 11 p.m. or later. The doctor told Dave it would be several hours before I would be transported and settled into a hospital room in Santa Maria. They advised him to go home. They promised to call him once I was there and settled in. The staff wheeled me to the area for parking lot pick-up, and the doctor gave the two young ladies on duty in the ambulance an overview of the situation. It was a bit unnerving witnessing the blank stare on the driver's face and hearing her ask the doctor a question, to which the answer was, "What I just told you."

She gave a little laugh and said, "Oh yeah, you just said that."

Well, it was the middle of the night, and she was probably resting when she got the call. The whole situation felt surreal, and I could not believe this was happening to me. I have felt this way since the moment I was diagnosed. Like this, cancer could not really be real. Still, it kept proving me wrong.

Once I was loaded up, we made the twenty-five-mile ride to the hospital, which was bumpy at times. I listened to the low voices of the young woman driver and her partner up front, which was somewhat comforting. It was the wee hours of the morning when I got to the hospital and settled into my own room. A call was placed to Dave to assure him I was there and being monitored. All I could think about was how whatever they gave me for this headache while still in Lompoc was not cutting it. They gave me some type of aspirin or painkiller and encouraged me to rest. Unfortunately, the rest was hard to come by. If the nurses were not in my room checking my vitals, which was necessary but intrusive, I was anticipating their next arrival. Somehow, the night passed.

In the morning, with the shift change, I met the nurses who would care for me throughout the day. They are so kind and sympathetic to my discomfort. I asked, "Isn't there something you can give me for this headache?"

At this point, none of the painkillers they gave me had even come close to curing it. They finally gave me a shot of morphine through my IV. You can't imagine the relief. Maybe now I could get some rest. Soon, though, Dave was there to see me. I really didn't want company. My only desire was to rest undisturbed. However, he wouldn't heed my request that he go home. He settled himself into a chair against the wall and worked on clearing old emails off his phone. He got into a conversation with one of the nurses caring for me and learned that she used to live in our neighborhood, just one street from where we reside. It's a small world. The day passes. I have zero appetite and have to ask often for more morphine to keep that headache at bay.

We would later learn that the headache was most likely caused by the medication meant to prevent nausea that I had been on since my chemo treatment up north. I really had not had any nausea before or after taking it in the first place. I certainly had no intention of taking that medication anymore.

Late afternoon, Dave leaves to go home and promises to return in the morning. "Don't rush," I tell him; "you don't have to be here all the time." I slip into another night where I seek nothing but sleep in between the timely check-ins from the nurses. True to his word, Dave is back in the morning, settling into his chair.

This morning my doctor pays a visit. He is followed in by his nurse, and his first words to me are, "What are you doing here?"

Up to this point, I had been a model patient with no serious complaints or additional issues outside the status quo. I didn't know what to say aside from explaining how I had taken a turn for the worse and describing the horrendous headache that continued to be an issue. He and Dave spoke a bit before he left to check on other patients, assuring us he would monitor my progress. Sleep was still what I wanted most, along with the pain medication. I did not yet have an appetite or the desire to put forth an effort to talk with anyone.

Sometime that afternoon, my cell phone rang, and Dave answered it. It was one of the employees from the financial institution I worked at. He was trying to reach me to let me know a group of employees had gathered and put together something on my behalf. It was there at the office for me to pick up whenever I was ready.

Tyler came to visit me that evening. One of his college courses was in Santa Maria, so after class ended, he drove to the hospital. He entered the room and stood by my bed, looking down at me, seemingly at a loss. Tyler is a quiet young man by nature, and at this moment, he seemed unable to speak at all.

I imagine seeing his normally nonstop mother lying listlessly in a hospital bed was unsettling. I didn't have the energy to say much. Dave and the nurse we had befriended were deep in conversation, and Tyler took a seat next to Dave. I wanted to ask him to come to hold my hand, knowing I would surely find strength through his touch, but I didn't want to interrupt the conversation between Dave and the nurse. The opportunity soon passed. There have been and continue to be so many times I wish I had spoken up and asked him to take my hand and hold it during that moment.

Shortly after, the two of them leave, and another night is upon me as I try to settle into it. The dark and quiet room is comforting. Soon, though, I hear music coming from somewhere outside. Making my way to the window, I see my room is parallel to a residential area. The sounds must be coming from someone's house or apartment. So much for the quiet I have so desperately been waiting for. It is a chore to tune out the intrusion.

Chapter Ten
Stem Cell Collection

The following morning, my third day there, I had a hankering for coffee but still not much of an appetite. The coffee, while not quite as good as mine at home, started to hit the spot, and I asked for another cup. The nurses are quick to oblige, my appreciation so apparent. As I mentioned earlier, I live for the coffee I drink every morning, curled up on the couch in the darkness before dawn. I now enjoy this cup while giving thanks to God for the care I am being given and reflecting on life a little. That which is behind me while pondering what may lie ahead. The situation at hand obviously didn't make for mornings of pleasant reflection or anticipation, but hey, the worst of times makes for a better appreciation of the better ones. My headache had passed, and I was starting to feel a bit of energy coming back into my body.

Dave came later in the morning, and we heard that my blood counts were coming back up, close to where they needed to be, to allow the hospital to discharge me safely. Crossing our fingers, we waited for the doctor to clear me. Dave was pushing me to try eating something, and I thought maybe some soup would be nice. He let the staff know, and while he was out, my lunch arrived. Again, I do not like to complain, but this is some of the worst soup I've ever had. It was so salty and unsatisfying. It was at this point I started feeling a little sorry for myself. Here my appetite has returned just a little, after eating nothing for almost three days, and what do I get?? Sucky soup. It gets set aside, and I enjoyed the milk and crackers that came with it instead.

Later in the afternoon, Dave returned, and we were visiting when I started feeling nauseous. Prior to this point in this journey, I had not once felt sick to my stomach, yet I know now I'm going to be sick, and I welcome it. Three days with nothing in my system but a little milk and crackers, along with intravenous pain medication, was taking its toll. Looking forward to the relief I would feel if I could just make it to the bathroom in time (I did), I shut the door and went to my knees at the toilet. The physical release felt so good. Still, all I wanted to do was go home.

I was feeling a bit better by then and watched a little television that evening once visiting hours were over. I still was not cleared to go home. Another night came and went. The following day, my appetite was better, and I ordered breakfast. It was far better than the lunch from the day before, and my energy was returning. Dave showed up, and we waited impatiently for my doctor to check in and send me home.

My doctor never did show up that morning. We had only seen him the one time he came in on my second day there. Many other emergencies to attend to, we're sure. Finally, though, the doctor was able to communicate to the staff that I was good to go, and we started packing up to leave. It was this last morning, day number four, and all this time without so much as a shower, that I found behind a curtain in the bathroom of my room that there had been a shower, along with little personal hygiene products, at my disposal this whole time. *Geez!! Who knew?* Oh well, it wasn't like I was ever in the mood or condition to shower safely by myself while I was there anyway.

We just wanted to get out of there. I was emotionally drained. Dave tried cheering me up by letting me know he had picked up the package my coworkers had put together for me the day before, and it was waiting for me at home. I put my mind on that and the long, hot shower I would take as soon as we got there.

We arrived home. I went into our bedroom and sat on the bed. Dave brought me the gift bag from my work group and told me to open it now. He also wanted me to know that when he picked it up, the employee who had called us while we were at the hospital had tears in his eyes when he handed the bag off to him while asking how I was. That was so touching to hear, and so nice to know that people genuinely cared.

Inside the bag was a card of encouragement signed by many employees from numerous branches. Though I had not even met many of these employees, there had been conversations between myself and most of them throughout the course of business. I could almost hear their voices as I read what they had written inside. It was as if they were reading their kind words of encouragement off that card to me as I sat on the bed. This moved me in a way I still can't explain. There was also a generous check in the card. A gathering of funds from these thoughtful coworkers to help Dave and me out with the multitude of expenses we were facing. There was a petal diffuser in the bag they hoped would be a calming source for me and some other little goodies to go along with it. Dave sat with me as I opened all these things, smiling and commenting on how good it must make me feel to know how many people truly cared about me.

It really did, and it was touching to him to hear me read aloud the lines in the card people wrote to me. He suggested I write a very heartfelt thank-you to all of them. I wholeheartedly agreed, put together a heartfelt thank-you to them in an email, and sent it to one of the employees to forward to everyone.

From there, it was straight to the shower. Oh, how good it felt to stand under that hot water after almost four days without showering. My hair, once wet, felt like a heavy weight pulling down on my head. I had known for several days before my hospital stay that it was on its way out. My scalp had been sensitive the days before and during that stay. To say my hair hurt was not an exaggeration. It hung limp on my head like a wet blanket, obviously dead due to the chemo. As I said before, I have been obsessed with how my hair looks for a long time. I curled it every day and spent a ridiculous amount of time styling and spraying it each morning before leaving the house. I wanted it to look perfect all the time.

I finished up and wrapped a towel around my head. I figured it would start coming out as soon as I started combing it. It did, in clumps. One more insult to add to the injuries I had been through in the past few days.

Strangely enough, I felt a surge of anger. In some sort of act of revenge, I decided to paint my fingernails in a nice clear coat of polish. I did so carefully while listening to some of my favorite music by Olivia Newton-John. It seemed fitting to be listening to her at this moment, she being a cancer survivor herself. This small act of self-indulgence did make me feel a little bit better. That is until I sat admiring my handiwork and discovered a long strand of my hair polished and dried onto one of my fingernails. Cancer's way, I guess, of being sure it got the last word in.

I believe it was late afternoon this same day that we got a call from the head nurse at my oncologist's office to report that my blood counts were where they needed to be for me to undergo the collection of stem cells for the transplant. I was to get to the hospital up north as soon as possible. The following day (Friday), we headed out to make my early Saturday morning appointment in the apheresis room at the hospital.

We had made hotel reservations sometime back for this time frame in expectation of this process. It had been a challenge as we did not know precisely when my blood levels would be up to par, only a guesstimate of around May 2nd. We had to have lodging and pay for it beginning on that date, whether we were there or not. The collection of stem cells is a process that generally takes anywhere from three to five days.

This would supply enough stem cells for the upcoming transplant and a backup supply that the hospital would freeze and store should I ever need to have this procedure done again.

We pulled into our hotel. The room provided a kitchen, a little sitting area, TV, and a bed. The "by the water" description it was advertised under turned out to be a foul-smelling swamp area. It did at least have a path to walk on next to it that we could take advantage of when we needed to get out of the room.

The following morning, we arrived at the hospital and parked in the parking lot there since it was the weekend. First on the list, when I checked in, was to test my blood to confirm that my blood levels were still where they needed to be for the apheresis.

The blood sample would have to be taken by courier to a lab for testing, and since pick-up would not be for a while, we had time to kill. Dave and I asked the nurse there where a good place would be to have breakfast close by, and we headed out to find the restaurant she recommended. It was quite a task finding it, and we were disappointed that they were not open for business yet once we did. We chose a little coffee shop in a strip mall some ways away and relaxed until we got the call from the nurse in the apheresis room. They had received my bloodwork results and said we were good to return to the hospital and get started. What we didn't know was that an annual parade had begun its festivities in the local area, and there were many detours along the route back. Our GPS, of course, did not consider those detours when trying to get us back.

Given that we were in an unfamiliar area, it was a long, very stressful journey back. When we arrived at the hospital an hour and a half later than expected, the staff said they had wondered what had happened to us. We explained what happened and then settled in for what was to come.

I was hooked up through the port in my chest to a tube connected to a machine that spins the blood being drawn from my body. I was the only patient in the apheresis room; it was dim, and the white noise coming from the machine as it worked made for a quiet, calming environment. This process would take several hours. I was anxious to get back to a book I'd started, and I encouraged Dave to take advantage of one of the comfortable chairs in the room that provides a little personalized TV set. The hours passed quietly, and we were done with the first collection. We returned to the hotel room to wind down for the day.

We later got a call from the hospital staff telling us that they were able to gather way more stem cells than what was required just in that one sitting. So, rather than needing between three to five appointments over as many days as we had expected this process to take, we were told I would not need to return at all. What a pleasant surprise. Not to mention less money spent on lodging. Dave had a group text going between all his siblings to keep them posted on our progress, and he reported the good news. *What a stud,* his little sister texted back to us all. We went to sleep that night, looking forward to an early start back home in the morning.

Upon leaving, we reached out to Dave's sister in Watsonville, and she arranged for her family to meet us for lunch at a resort in Aptos. Though feeling self-conscious about walking into this big, bright, beautiful room wearing a baseball cap to cover my head, where but a few wisps of my hair remained, I knew it was something I would have to get used to. After all, soon, I would be completely bald. We approached the table her family was seated at.

"Hi, cutie," was Michele's greeting. God bless those who love us and know how much a kind word at the right time means. We enjoyed a lovely meal overlooking a beautiful ocean view. Though I could not indulge in the refreshing, colorful cocktail Michele enjoyed, she assured me it was delicious. I was grateful for the things I could indulge in.

Once lunch was over, we said our goodbyes and headed home. It was May 6th, and my next scheduled appointment was May 16th. We would head back up north on May 15th. That would be the beginning of our extended stay, anywhere from three weeks to a month for the transplant. This meant nine days of unwanted time between now and the time we would head back north, and I am not looking forward to this. The only place I wanted to be was back at work, taking care of business. The fact that Dave was reporting to work every day only added to my misery.

During that time frame, I drove to the financial institution I worked for to do some banking, but I did not feel in the mood to visit my coworkers in the back office. I was low that day, as Tyler was planning on attending a junior college located fifty miles south of us, and he would be moving out. Classes were set to begin in early June, which meant he would be moving out for the first time in his life while we were up north for our extended stay. Tyler is our only child, and I felt like cancer was robbing Dave and me of that monumental moment in his life. One more bullet through my heart, waged in a war I never asked to fight, one in which I had never raised a weapon and had little to no ammunition to fight back with.

Suddenly, two women were bouncing around me with big smiles on their faces, giggling as they hugged me, planting little kisses on my cheeks.

These were two long-time employees from another department at my work, whom I have been close with for a very long time. They just happened to be finishing their daily walk around the block when they saw me at the entrance of the building. It was enough to lift my spirits. I even changed my mind about visiting the employees in my department to say hi. God works in wonderful little ways.

Months later, I would pull both women aside to tell them just how much their gestures meant to me that day.

Chapter Eleven
Chemo Infusions

During another one of those days while at home, before the transplant, but after losing my hair, my sister, Jeanette, and I went to a financial institution to try to take care of some of the financial needs of our parents' estate. I had decided to wear my wig as I would be in a public and professional setting. I struggled to put it on, and while I did the best I could with what little experience I had with this kind of thing, it just didn't feel quite right when I left the house. As Jeanette and I sat before the young lady at the bank, who was assisting us with our questions, I continually felt the need to apologize for the appearance of my hair.

I tried to say things out loud to Jeanette concerning my wig so the young lady there would get somewhat of an idea of my situation. Each time I expressed concern and tugged on it, this kind person would say, "Oh, no worries, you're good."

Finally, exasperated with my nervous chit-chat, Jeanette took a good look at me and said, "Well, no wonder it doesn't feel right, silly, you have it on crooked!"

Unbeknownst to me, a small elastic tab was sewn up under the front of the wig, which should have been situated in the middle of my forehead so the hair would fall evenly on both sides. Instead, I had everything pulled to one side, so the tab and my entire head of hair were crooked. Well, this was all new to me, and I didn't remember the detail of the elastic tab coming up when I bought the wig. It would take me some time and practice to get this stuff right.

I must have gotten pretty good at it, as one day, much later, I went in for one of my checkups with my primary care physician, who I had been seeing for some twenty-plus years, and he went to check my ears. I said, "Oh, just a second," and went to adjust the elastic band holding the hair on my wig over my ears.

He chuckled momentarily, admitting he hadn't even realized I was wearing a wig. How's that for picking out a wig close to my natural color and style and learning to put it on properly!? Again, he knows me quite well, and in fact, he had delivered Tyler. He also took a moment on that day to commend me for not trying to delay Tyler's departure for college by laying a guilt trip on him for leaving home during my time of need.

"Oh, hell no," I said. "I will not allow Tyler's life to be delayed in any way, shape, or form because of my cancer. That just ain't happening!!!"

After Jeanette and I had finished up at the bank, we went to a local clothing store, since I would need some comfortable clothes to wear during my extended stay at the hotel during the transplant and while at home on disability. I had never had much luck shopping for clothes before, but her offer was an expected treat, and I was excited. Having my big sister there to pick out clothes for me to try on, approve or disapprove of, turned out to be not only fun but victorious, too. I felt like I'd hit the lottery. I purchased quite a few clothes that day, some of which I still wear.

Mother's Day 2018 was the first Mother's Day my mother was not here for us to honor. There was a celebration planned at my sister and brother-in-law's house to celebrate many of us mothers, and it was an enjoyable occasion. Toward the end of the day, the Pickles women presented me with a large plastic tub full of wrapped gifts. Enough for me to have one to open every day during the three to four weeks we would be staying at the hotel during the transplant process. There was also a goodie bag for Dave. It included such things as Beer Nuts, Beef Jerky, I think, a cigar, and some other guy stuff. We were touched beyond words. Everyone gave us farewell hugs, prayers, and heartfelt well wishes, as this would be our last visit before Dave and I headed north on the 15th.

There would be one more surprise put together for us by the family before we left. We were presented with a Costco card for $600 to stock our hotel room with groceries. That was $100 from each couple in the Pickles clan. Wow!! No way were we going hungry. On top of all this, our niece, Kamille, was working on making and selling T-shirts with the saying: "Certified Badass in the fight against cancer," and below those words was the slogan #TeamSandra. Each day we were gone, one family member or friend would text Dave a picture of themselves wearing that shirt. We got some great shots. Even pets were sporting the attire.

We checked into our hotel on the evening of the 15th of May. I was scheduled the following day for blood work at the infusion treatment center, a chest X-Ray at the cancer center, and later for a meeting with my doctor and her nurse coordinator. They informed

Dave and me of more information about what was coming. It seemed so overwhelming. Again, all I really wanted to do was get started with this so I could be done with it. The in-between things were something I was just going to have to deal with. Then I could get back to my real life.

We wrapped things up with my appointment and used the time left on this day to go to Costco. We used our gift card to stock the hotel room with three to four weeks of groceries.

We bought all kinds of food. Some things we had never tried before. I got some healthy drinks I had never tasted, and Dave was excited to try the stuffed green peppers we had stumbled upon, which looked so enticing. I enjoyed making stuffed green peppers and cabbage rolls at home. These peppers looked good with their meat, rice, and cheese mixture. What we couldn't know at the time we were shopping off the hook with our big-ticket gift card was that the majority of our time there, I would have little to no appetite. Most of our time there, just the sight or smell of food made me nauseous.

Dave could not even tempt me with Cream of Wheat in those days. There was also the fact that Dave took advantage of the complimentary breakfast buffet there every day. Thank God he had that outlet and an opportunity to get out of that room and have some quiet time on his own. However, it did alleviate the need to use up some of those groceries. It turned out that most of the food we bought was either given to some of the hotel staff when we left or eventually went to waste.

We had baked a couple of those stuffed green peppers in the early days of our stay, and they were good, filling the room with a delicious aroma.

However, in the days after the transplant, when I was listless and hypersensitive to those smells, I asked that Dave not bake them again. It's strange how some things stay with you during traumas such as these. Not only did I not want to see or smell those peppers during our stay, but that sentiment also lingered with me for a long time after we got home. I could no longer look at those same peppers in our local Costco or agree to Dave buying and bringing them home. When he eventually did and put them in the oven to bake, the smell was tolerable, but I could not eat much of one. I'm not even sure how I would feel about one now.

May 17th came, the day I would receive the first of the two rounds of an intravenous chemo drip I had to receive before the transplant. The line was hooked up to my port, and I tried to relax as best I could. At this stage of the game, I was getting accustomed to sitting for long hours. I was getting in a lot of reading.

Dave went off to find a way to pass the time. I was sitting in the infusion room, which was quite crowded, hooked up to my IV stand, which, of course, was plugged into the wall when I had to get up to use the restroom. I unplugged the IV stand and went in search of an available bathroom. Along the way, I ran into one of my fellow transplant patients. She was part of the original group Dave and I had our first class with, the only one I kept in touch with in the years following our transplants. I learned she was having a rough day. She was exhausted, suffering from nausea, and running out of steam. We took a moment to compare our symptoms and console each other. Soon, I was in the restroom behind locked doors when the shrill sounds of a fire alarm began.

At first, I was convinced it was an alarm caused by my unplugging my IV stand from the wall, and I was horrified. Soon enough, though, the anxious voice of one of the nurses could be heard verifying that this was yet another fire alarm.

At this point, I leaned forward, laid my head on my knees as I sat on the toilet, and laughed. "Boy," I thought, "I must be 'hot stuff.'" The only two fire alarms this hospital has had in years and years took place only when I was in the building. There was also the relief that the alarm did not result from my unplugging my IV stand. I finished up my business and returned to my chair.

There was a woman in the infusion room playing the harp. I had noticed her several times in various hospital areas throughout my visits. The music was beautiful and calming.

One of the first things you see when you enter this hospital is a glorious piano in the middle of the lobby with a person seated at it playing soft and soothing music. So generous of those who provide these simple pleasures for the sole purpose of calming those who are suffering. Another thing I have noticed while there in the infusion rooms is a woman who comes around and gives short, little neck and shoulder massages to the patients. I watched, envious of those patients lucky enough to get her attention. Well, today must be my lucky day because she approached me and asked if I would like a massage.

"Oh, yes," I replied.

She worked gently on my neck and upper shoulders. It felt so relaxing, though I kept wishing she would dig harder into my tense muscles. We completed our necessary duties for the day, received a new IV fluid bag, and headed back to the hotel room for the night.

The next day is a break between the two chemo treatments, and the only things we need to do at the hospital are a blood draw and a change out of the IV fluid bag. Still, the drive from the hotel to the hospital was always time-consuming and challenging because of the traffic.

The following day, we returned for my second round of chemo. This treatment requires the patient to chew on and swallow ice chips for a minimum of twenty minutes before being administered. This lessens the damage to the gums and esophagus this particular drug is prone to do. I dutifully follow instructions. Again, this is a drip that takes hours: another opportunity for me to read and another chore for Dave to find a way to kill time. We get through the day, and when we're done, we return to our tiny home away from home.

I reported to the hospital the day before the transplant for blood draws and to have my fluid bag changed. On our way through the halls of the hospital, we ran into one of the gals that had been in our introductory class and who was also preparing for her stem cell transplant. We stopped for a moment to chat and compare experiences. She is entirely bald by this time and wears no covering on her head. I envy her courage. I do not have the guts to go without the little gray cap that people say compliment my blue eyes, which I wear under a dark blue baseball cap. There are still wisps of straggly hair that hang here and there on my head.

I asked her how she handled the last two rounds of chemo. She says she only had one of the two I recently had. When I asked why, she explained they told her that since she used to be a smoker, it was better not to administer one of those medications.

"I used to be a smoker," I say, "in fact, for sixteen years. Why, then, was it given to me?"

She, of course, had no explanation. After our pleasantries, Dave and I continued down the halls on our way to whatever destination it was we were looking for at the moment. Long after that time, while reviewing my medical records online, I learned I was listed as never having been a smoker. *Wait ... what??*

There are waiting areas all along the way in this hospital, and when passing one, I see a very tall, slim young lady who is completely bald and all alone. She sits on one of the cushioned benches, then lies across it, resting her head across her arms. She looks so very disheartened. "Why," my heart cried, "is this young woman all alone? No one should be going through what she was going through alone."

I wanted to stop and hold her in my arms and tell her I knew what she was going through. That maybe, if only for a moment, everything was going to be alright, even though I, of course, had no idea if it really would be. I lacked the energy to be supportive of anyone. As it was, Dave was my only source of strength at the time, and my entire support system rested on his shoulders. Other patients from my group had spouses, siblings, and other various friends and family members who could be present at multiple times for them. Since we were so far from home, Dave was on duty 24/7. I couldn't ask him to spare any energy he may have had at the time to comfort someone else.

So, I passed by this sad young woman, ashamed that my eyes were cast down as I did. She could not have known that it was the only way I could walk past her. I had a flashback then of a moment during one of our first trips to the hospital, where I had spotted a tiny wisp of a girl sitting on a cushioned bench in the lobby. She sat alone, with her arms tightly wrapped around her knees, which were drawn up to her chest. She rested her head on top of her knees. She made for such a small, sad picture. I recall admiring the pretty green sweater she was wrapped in. Still, that lovely sweater wasn't enough to thaw the loneliness shivering through her thin shoulders.

Chapter Twelve
Stem Cell Transplant

May 21st was my transplant day. Ironically, this was the date of the month and day we had lost my sister Linda, forty-six years prior. According to the medical staff, it would now be my new birthday. May 21st was also the date I was involved in a minor traffic accident in the town we live in some years ago. While the accident wasn't serious, and no one was hurt, it did total the Toyota Corolla I depended on to last me for many more years to come. When I told my sister, Barbara, about the accident and the correlation of the date, her response was, "When you mention this incident to Mother, do not mention the date it happened." I was very cautious not to.

Lab results were in, things looked good, and the transplant will be a go today. The procedure will basically be done the same way the chemo drugs were administered. The bag of stem cells that had been thawed out from their frozen state would be hooked up to an IV line, inserted into the port in my chest, and pumped back into my body. Hopefully, they would bring some healthy life back into it.

I lay in bed in a private room where the nurse prepared the IV lines for hookup. She moved about with confidence. While she was not tall, her back and shoulders were straight and sturdy, and her focus was razor-sharp, making her somewhat of a giant in my eyes. Dave watched her work and, out of curiosity, asked her how long the transplant would take.

"Seven minutes," she answers.

Dave and I are both speechless. For all that had taken place in our lives in these past seven months since my diagnosis and all the preparation it took to get to this moment, it seemed incomprehensible that the last piece of this puzzle would be completed with a seven-minute procedure.

Seeing our surprised expression, the nurse nodded and said, "Yes, anywhere between seven to ten minutes."

Wow!!

That being said, things get started. The nurse warned me that some patients who have undergone this procedure claim they get a taste in their mouth like creamed corn. I only smelled something slightly sweet. Dave says the room had an aroma that smelled like fruit and tomatoes. Though I was unaware of it, he claims he could smell it for days afterward in the truck, the hotel room, and even the bathroom. The transplant process moved quickly; the nurse was at my bedside the entire time and gently squeezed the bag of cells as it emptied, making sure everything made it through. Then she unhooked the IV line and moved the IV pole from my room.

Within minutes, a group of hospital staff was at the foot of my bed with a little pink cake that said "Happy Birthday," and they all sang "Happy Birthday" to me. Dave and I smiled through the song and thanked them. Food was, though, the last thing I wanted to see. I had a feeling this cute little cake would go to waste, and it did eventually end up untouched and in the trash.

We went back to the hotel, which would continue to be home for another three weeks. I needed to report to the hospital daily for blood work and a check of my vitals.

The morning after the transplant, I got up to go to the restroom and, upon standing, felt an immediate panic that I may not make it to the toilet before, amongst other things, vomiting. I shut the bathroom door, hoping to share as little of this experience with Dave as possible. He lingered outside and asked if I was okay. I got through some dreadful experiences before allowing him in. He came in and went to his knees at my side, rubbing my back as I kneeled beside the toilet and got sick again. While I hadn't thought I wanted him in there, the gentle pressure on my back and his presence made me feel better than I anticipated.

Dave had asked one of the nursing staff at the hospital if he should be worried about using the same bathroom as me. Since my chemo infusions had started, we had been somewhat concerned about any lingering effects the drugs may have in the air and on the toilet seat when I used it. The gentleman we spoke with did suggest we use a bathroom cleaner or wipes containing bleach to wipe the toilet down well each time I used it. Dave was careful to see it was done.

On day two after the transplant, while I was in a chair in the infusion room, I was encouraged to take one of the potassium pills I had been prescribed and was given some water to help wash it down. These pills are pretty large and hard to swallow. I managed to choke it down, but was immediately overwhelmed by a wave of nausea, and I felt an intense desire to vomit in order to relieve the sensation. The nurse assisting me recognized this and squeezed two points at the base of my skull with her fingers. The feeling eventually dissipated. This was the first time I experienced that sensation, and I hope it will be the last. I got through the day, and we returned to the hotel.

The following day, I found that my vision was blurry. When Dave mentioned this to the nurses during our visit that day, they explained that the chemotherapy drug I'd been given the day before contained steroids that tend to stimulate cataract growth, ultimately affecting one's vision.

Great!! So, on top of all this shit, now I am not going to be able to see or read. We also mentioned the nausea that had been lingering since the treatment was administered. One of the nurses perked up and was quick to arrange for a prescription to be given to us for a medication that should alleviate my discomfort.

It seemed like they prescribed me something new every day, and we went to the local Walgreens in town for more meds after my appointments. The shelf of the dresser in our hotel room looked like a pharmacy. Dave took a picture of all the pills on the shelves and sent it out on the group text. We had a list of all the medications I was on, which explained what each one was for, how much I needed to take, and how often I needed to take it.

Passing the time in a small room with just a little kitchen, a bed, an uncomfortable couch, and a TV is challenging at best. I, of course, could not leave the room without my respirator, and I hated wearing it. We did venture out a couple of times to walk the path alongside that stinky swamp area next to the hotel. On one of those walks, we passed by a couple pushing a toddler in a stroller, and surprisingly, the little boy looked up at me and smiled. It made me feel pretty good, as I thought he would be scared of me with that apparatus on my face. Later, when I proudly mentioned to Dave that the little guy smiled at me, he said, "That's because he thought you were Darth Vader."

I couldn't help but laugh. "Wow, thanks a lot," I replied.

I also got a good giggle one morning when, after showering and trying to get myself together, Dave was hanging about inside the bathroom, looking like he had something on his mind. However, he was hesitant to speak up. When I looked at him and asked, "What?" he said, "Honey, I just gotta ask. What are you using the crème rinse that's in the shower for? You don't have any hair," he reminded me.

I laughed. Like, I didn't know that? My scalp often had a stinging sensation about it, and applying the rinse to it allowed me to rub my head gently with a thick, soothing crème. Besides that, it smelled good, and I was determined to enjoy any small pleasure I could find.

As he continued trying to keep my spirits up during that dismal time, there came his offer one day while he sat looking at me with a smirk on his face. When I asked him what was funny, he said, "I was just thinking of asking you if I could run my fingers through your hair."

I giggled but tried to look serious as I gave him what we affectionately refer to as "the look."

He just looked at me and laughed some more, saying, "The look" just didn't have the same effect when I had no hair.

A few days after the transplant, I told Dave the tops of my shoulders had been itchy for the past couple of days and asked if he would take a look at them. He checked them and said there were a bunch of little red bumps on them that looked like some sort of rash. We assumed it was a reaction to the medications. I had Dave apply some lotion to them, which was somewhat soothing.

While I didn't feel so bad the first week after the transplant, the medical staff had warned me that it would be around nine to thirteen days after the procedure that the stem cells would start to graph and that I would notice a change in how I felt. They were not kidding. It is probably just about the ninth day in, and all I want is to be immersed in darkness and complete silence and left alone to sleep. During this time, though, I must still go to the hospital every day and have my blood drawn. I simply do not want to move. I could hear Dave's voice softly saying, "I know you don't want to hear this, honey, but I need to get you up, so I can get you to the hospital."

Not only did I not want to hear this, but the thought of moving was inconceivable to me. Still, I knew no matter how hard it would be or how heavy my body and soul were, I had to pull myself up out of those dark shadows and allow Dave to help me up and out of that bed.

My first destination was the bathroom, then into the shower. I then took a minute to apply some foundation and blush to my face. "You don't have to do all that," Dave would say. "Just go as you are."

But I did have to go through those motions, if for no one else but me. A shower in the morning was how I started every day and what helped me clear my mind a bit and come alive. I just couldn't face the world without a little makeup, and it only took a couple of minutes after my shower to make me feel ready. I would then put on my little gray cap and top it off with my blue baseball cap before putting my respirator on to go from the hotel room to the truck. These short trips to the hospital drained me. Again, it was more than just the drive with all the traffic. It was also the journey from the parking lot to the parking lot elevator, then through the crowds to the bus stop, standing and waiting for the next bus to go to the hospital lobby and then checking in for labs. Then, back to the entrance to wait for the next bus to make the return trip back to the parking lot, so we could make our way back to the hotel when we were done. Dave was continually on me to put my respirator on. While I hated wearing that thing, there were many other people in and around the hospital areas wearing them, so I at least did not feel alone.

During those days, the only thing Dave had to do was watch TV. He is not a reader like I am, and it was on continuously, facing the bed where I was trying to sleep. Every time a commercial came on for food, especially fast food, and there were many of them, showing giant dripping hamburgers and salty fries, I felt nauseous. I could eat nothing, no matter how much Dave tried to encourage me. Our room was on the hotel's first floor and just down the hall from the breakfast buffet. Dave would visit it every morning. I was so thankful he had those meals to go to and that time to himself, away from the dark environment I craved in our room. The downside was with the buffet being so close, the smell permeated my senses. The sight, smell, and even the thought of food made me sick. I lost about thirteen pounds during our stay, though it could have been much worse. I know many people lose much more weight than that under these types of circumstances.

When I was most listless and going in for my checkups, Dave and I were most appreciative of a particularly exuberant young man working in the cancer ward named Brian. He cheered me on each time he saw me drag myself in and exclaimed, "Ohhh, Ms. Pickles, you're going to start feeling better pretty soon. You just wait and see Ms. Pickles. It's going to be soon now!"

The listless expression on my face, and the apparent state of my exhaustion, had to be more than enough evidence that his words were hard for me to take to heart at the time. Yet he stood by my side as I was hooked up to my IV, patiently monitoring any air bubbles that appeared in the lines, and kept up with his kind words of encouragement. It was hard to fathom ever feeling better in my waking moments during those days.

There, of course, finally did come a day when I started to feel some energy seeping back into my veins. Then the patient Brian saw coming in was a bit perkier and had a little more color to her cheeks. He noticed those changes as I headed his way up the hall. He excitedly called to me in cheers that echoed through the corridors, "Ohhh, Ms. Pickles, I told you that you were going to start feeling better soon. Didn't I tell you, Ms. Pickles, that it would be real soon!?"

You could not be around this young man and not feel his infectious joy. Through the darkest of those days, I could hear his voice booming in my brain and knew he was somewhere out there cheering me on. Dave and I looked forward to seeing him each day, and we shared our stories about him with family and friends upon our return home. He is someone we will never forget.

We are now around two weeks past the day of the transplant and have at least another week we'll have to stay in the motel to be near the hospital. We continue with the daily routine. We were, of course, anxious to get to the end of our stay, get out of that small room, and back to the comforts of our own home. Every day that went by, it seemed more challenging to pass the time.

Finally, the time came to go to the hospital and look at removing the port from my chest and hopefully be discharged to go home. There was some type of concern when I got to the hospital to undergo minor surgery to remove the port that threatened to delay us. However, I can't quite recall what it was. What I do remember was how apprehensive and frustrated we were that we may not be able to go home the following morning.

To our great relief, they were able to go through with the procedure. Though it was somewhat painful, I was grateful to take the discomfort in order for it to be done and over with. Afterward, we returned to the hotel and started packing in anticipation of our departure. Hallelujah.

Chapter Thirteen

Isolation

We were on our way! We both soaked up some relief with each mile that passed behind us in our rearview mirror, though we knew this journey would by no means end at our driveway. It would simply be the beginning of the healing process from a procedure that would not end this incurable disease but be an attempt to better manage it.

We arrived back in town. We stopped at the beauty salon where my two sisters-in-law work, as they had our house key. Our nieces had volunteered to clean the house well before our return home, so we left the key with the family. Though I am self-conscious about getting out of the truck with my respirator on and going into, of all places, a beauty salon, I do want to see my sisters-in-law and let them know I am somewhat okay.

Back in our own environment, I take refuge in the bedroom that serves as my sanctuary. Dave settles us in, and while I feel better than

I did in the earlier days, I have a long way to go. He will, of course, return to work in the following days, and I will again be home alone.

Every evening he prepares my daily medications in a pill organizer, and every morning gives them to me. He then showers and dresses for work before returning to the bedside to kiss me goodbye.

There is nothing better than rest to heal the body and soul, and while I tried to appreciate the time I had to do this, I just wanted to be done with it.

My appetite was still almost nonexistent. In fact, I couldn't even stomach the thought of my coffee with my favorite sweet cream. A light warm tea with honey was about all that appealed to me to sip on.

Having no desire to eat was somewhat of a blessing at the time, as the round of chemo that had required me to chew and swallow ice for twenty minutes had left my esophagus so sore it hurt to swallow. This is still an issue for me at times, even three and a half years later. My mouth and gums were like raw hamburger meat. I used a mouthwash for dry mouth as often as I could tolerate it. At that time, it would have been painful to have food in my mouth and try to chew it.

My spirits were further dampened by the reflection of my body in the mirror. I knew I had lost weight, but I was still unprepared for what I saw in the bright light of my bathroom mirror. I believe most women have an area on their body where it is more difficult to lose weight than in other places, and for me, it is my thighs. My skin now lay like layers of crepe paper on their insides, and my midsection was so emaciated I had to avert my eyes from the mirror.

Avoiding my reflection became the norm for me for some time after that. How ironic that I had been living my life for so long, always trying to avoid weight gain, while thinking, "It would be but a dream come true if I ever needed to gain weight." Like most of us,

I enjoy eating. Not only that, but it would also be so great to splurge without guilt on all the goodies I always passed on.

In so many ways, I was learning that you need to be careful what you wish for in this life. For years I had wanted perfect, no-fuss hair. Now I was bald. No hair to fuss with there. How I wanted, for even one day, to eat anything and everything I wanted to in vast amounts and not worry about gaining weight. Now I needed to gain weight and had no appetite. There was also the fact that all the things I had dreamed of gorging on were sweets or rich foods laden with fats and carbohydrates, which poison the health of a person with cancer. Word on the streets was "sugar feeds cancer."

I can't say it was too difficult being home in isolation for the first thirty days after the transplant. I had little energy, no appetite to fuel my body, and not much desire to step outside the house since I couldn't do so without my respirator on. I hated that thing and would be damned if I was going to let anyone else see me in it if I could help it. My niece Rachel's husband worked locally in law enforcement. I would tease her in a text one day about how if I dared to walk the streets of my neighborhood with my respirator on, he would be the first officer to get the call from worried neighbors, wondering who or what was walking around along their streets. I surely would have been concerned if I saw someone walking around looking like that.

I allowed one of my best friends, Marla, over for a brief visit, calling out to her to wait while I put on my respirator before she entered. I was comfortable enough with her to show her my bald head. She was so sympathetic, acknowledging the fact that she knew how much my hair had meant to me. Dave had mentioned that I had handled losing all my hair much better than he had expected me to. I thought so too. Truth be told, by this time, my feelings had been rubbed so raw that I was too numb to feel emotional about much of anything. This separation from self and reality seemed a necessary evil for me then. Unfortunately, while they joined back together as time went on, there have been, and continue to be, so many times I have to go back to that place of separation.

It's called survival.

So, here I was, housebound and miserable. I am not a daytime TV watcher, and while I love to read, instead of reading books for pleasure, I found myself on the computer reading procedures related to my job, hoping to be better prepared to get back to work. I also needed to be more confident about filling my role as supervisor. I figured the more I read, the better I would be when I returned to it. Another thing I would do to pass the time was spend hours listening to and watching music videos of my favorite songs on the computer. Since I love music and dancing, this was one of my most treasured past times during those days.

It was shortly after our return home, and prior to my thirty-day isolation ending, when Dave and I began getting really confused as to why I was sweating so much every night. Many mornings, I woke to drenched sheets, and Dave made me get up so he could strip the bed. I, of course, was of post-menopausal age and had been on hormones prescribed by my primary doctor for many years to control these effects. Still, during the class we attended at the hospital pretransplant, we were both under the impression we had been told the transplant would push me past menopause. So, I had not continued with those prescribed medications after the recommended hold on all drugs during the transplant expired. The rash on my shoulders that came about during our stay in the hotel became worse with the sweating, and I sometimes asked Dave to apply lotion on them.

After complaining to some of Dave's siblings about the night sweats I was having, his youngest sister and her friend went so far as to order a device to combat this type of problem. It was a wind machine made to fit under the sheets of your bed and deliver cool air while you sleep. Wow, who knew such a thing existed? I was touched by their generosity, and while I tried to make it work, I eventually gave up. It was either too cold, not cold enough, or so loud I couldn't sleep, and I already had issues sleeping.

One day, after my 30-day isolation ended, I was in the beauty salon where my two sisters-in-law work. I told one of them that I wished the few remaining strands of hair still hanging on my head would just go ahead and fall out. She ran to the station where the hairdresser worked and asked if she could help.

She was more than happy to oblige by using her clippers to completely shave my head and rid it of those wispy strands. The girl sitting at her station was looking our way with a somewhat perplexed look on her face. I would have been shocked, too, to see someone sitting still for this. I felt the need to let the reason I was doing this be known. I jokingly told the hairdresser the story about Dave asking me why I was using crème rinse on my bald head while we were in the hotel up north. I was sure to speak the name of the hospital where we went, which is quite well known for its cancer treatment, loud and clear in hopes that she would get the picture.

Before leaving work to go out on disability, I had learned that one of the gals that had worked in the department I had mentored in had the same type of cancer I have, as well as having had the same kind of stem cell transplant I'd had. She'd had hers done at a different hospital some ten years before this time, and she spent her thirty days in the hospital rather than as an outpatient as I had been. This employee worked in a different location than where I worked, so I didn't know her well, but she had given me her phone number and said to call her anytime if I needed to talk. I hesitated for a while, but knew it was time to connect for some support.

I called her, and she graciously shared her story and gave me hope and encouragement. I asked her if and when I would ever feel hungry again, and she assured me I would and probably soon. She answered many of my questions, and it was reassuring to hear it had been ten years since her transplant, with no signs of the disease showing back up again. Wow, the form I read and signed before my transplant gave a possible remission time of approximately two to five years. I scoffed at this when I read it, as I planned on being so healthy that it wouldn't show up until long after that. Hearing her story gave me more hope to reach that goal. She and I kept in touch for a while, mainly through text during my stay at home.

In those days, I was still under the illusion that my disability would just last between six and eight weeks. One of the things that had me believing this even more, was that the person at the hospital handling the disability paperwork for my claim had, in error, entered the date for my return to work as July 6th. This was less than six weeks after the transplant. This did seem kind of soon to me, but … okay. I also thought it rather odd that I would be reporting back to work on a Friday. Still, I didn't dwell on it. I wanted to get back to work as soon as possible, so I certainly wasn't going to complain or question it.

Later, when I ended up being out of work much longer than I had anticipated, there was a delay in collecting my disability monies while we resolved the issues of the incorrect dates being listed on the paperwork that had been provided to the Social Security office. It's a good thing Dave was receiving his regular income at the time. The person who had made the error on my paperwork apologized profusely, and I did feel bad for him too. After all, we all make mistakes.

Chapter Fourteen
Disability

It is June, and time for my 30-day follow-up. I am looking forward to meeting with my doctor, being cleared of having to wear this damn respirator, and asking her a couple of questions. One of the first concerns I talk about is that I am still sweating like crazy at night, and my shoulders are covered in that rash, made worse by the sweat, making it itch and burn. As noted earlier, I had stopped taking the hormone pills prescribed by my primary doctor, being under the impression transplant pushed me past menopause. When I explained this to the doctor, she looked at both of us with an expression on her face that clearly said, "Are you out of your minds?"

She then said, "The surgery does nothing of the sort," and Dave and I were both baffled as to how we were so clear about the information given to us at the initial meeting. My doctor advised me to start back on my hormone pills immediately and prescribed a steroid cream to help with the rash on my shoulders.

Geez, no wonder I am sweating every night now when I had not done so before. I was also looking forward to being cleared to indulge in a glass of wine, since alcohol has been prohibited for me for the past three months. While I am not a big drinker, I do enjoy a couple of cocktails or some wine on the weekends. I was under the impression that a bit of wine would be fine once I was thirty days out from surgery. The conversation that took place between Dave, me, the doctor, and her assistant was almost comical. My doctor has a bit of an accent which was not easy for me to understand, so her assistant worked as an interpreter of sorts between us all.

We went back and forth as I sheepishly asked if it would be okay for me to have a glass of wine that evening. We had plans to stay at Dave's sister Michele's house that night, and the idea of celebrating passing my 30-day follow-up with her with a glass of wine was pretty exciting to me. The assistant asks the doctor, who answers her, and then she asks me, "Are we talking red wine or white wine?"

"Probably white," I tell her.

She translates back to the doctor, who then asks her to ask us, "Are we talking six ounces or eight ounces?"

"Gee, I don't know; how ever many ounces a glass of wine is," I say.

The assistant and the doctor chat between themselves for another minute or two, and then the assistant tells me, "She says you can have a small glass of wine, but to be careful."

When the doctor's assistant sees my somewhat fallen face, she says, "Hey, if it were up to her, no one would ever drink again."

All righty, then.

Well, let me tell you, I would need more than one little glass of wine after hearing what came next in our conversation, which is my disability time, and the date I can return to work. When we tell the doctor that I am looking forward to returning to work on July 6th, she looks at us again with that "Are you out of your minds?" expression.

"July?? No way," was her and her assistant's response.

"What do you mean?" I asked. "That's what the paperwork on my disability claim says," I told her.

Another three-way conversation takes place, and they're made aware that there has been a mistake made by the person in their claims department. They informed us there was no way I could go back to work that soon.

"How soon can I go back?" I asked.

They ask me what kind of work is it that I do.

"I am a collections supervisor for a financial institution," I tell them.

"You have to avoid stress," my doctor says, "especially during the healing process, and with that kind of job, there is no way to avoid anxiety."

Well, even I couldn't argue with that. Still, when the doctor came back with no earlier than *September* as the date I could return, I was stunned. I mean, here we were in *June*. Three more months? No way!

"What if I work from home?" I asked, as this had been the plan discussed at work when I left.

"No," they said, "not even from home. It would still be too much stress."

I was beyond devastated. How could this be? September had not been part of the plan. Not even an entire bottle of red or white wine could have soothed that news that day. Dave and I left the doctor's office and climbed on a shuttle bus to return to the parking lot. As we walked to the truck, my mind swirled with thoughts on how to get around this.

"What if I do 'this'?" or "What if I do 'that'?" I thought out loud.

Finally, Dave pulled me to a stop in the parking garage and, holding me by the arm, through gritted teeth, said, "Sandra, let it go. With everything I've been through with you in the past few months, you will just have to let it go and stay home, like the doctor said. She has your best interest in mind, and she's trying to help you heal."

I knew he was right, even if I didn't want to admit it, and I didn't say another word as we got into the truck and began the drive to Michele's house. I did at least get to indulge in a glass of white wine with her that evening and had Dave take a picture of us together on the balcony of their home, which has a lake as its backdrop.

The bed we sleep in while we are there is a pull-out couch, which is located in the living room of their home. Since I am self-conscious about them waking up while I am still sleeping, coming up, and seeing me lying there with my bald head, I do my best to keep the thin gray cap on my head through the night. This isn't easy, as it makes me so warm it's hard for me to sleep. Still, I would rather sleep restlessly than be seen bald by anyone other than Dave.

During the first few months after the transplant, there were a number of things I had to avoid. I still had to follow a cautionary diet for the first thirty days. No fruit, especially berries, which, again, had been one of the core parts of my diet before all this, and one I really enjoyed. Other forbidden foods were bean and vegetable sprouts and foods that were not thoroughly cooked. I could not pick up after the dog when he did his business (darn). Dave was so gracious in walking him for me every night and cleaning up after him. I could not vacuum the house or be in a room that had been vacuumed for at least twenty minutes after the job had been done. This was not easy, as I like a clean house, and I enjoy cleaning. This was something I was supposed to avoid between two and six months.

There were many times I imposed on Tyler to do a run of the house with the vacuum while I was out walking the dog. I could not garden, care for houseplants, or be around birds or livestock. Another area of caution during some of this time was physical contact with your partner. Avoiding this did not seem like much of a sacrifice, as Dave and I had an overly emotional concern for one another.

So, as the physical contact decreased, the emotional connection increased. There is nothing like having someone at your side who truly meant it when they said, "I do."

We live in a small neighborhood where many of us know each other by sight, even if we don't know each other by name. Those of us who are regular dog walkers sometimes stop to chat. On one of my first ventures out after my 30-day quarantine, I ran into a friend that lit up with a smile as soon as she saw me. She told me I was the answer to so many of her prayers. I was so touched and thanked her over and over. Many were the neighbors I ran into on my walks who stopped to hug me and tell me how happy they were to see me. I didn't even know who all of them were.

Some said they couldn't believe how good I looked for having just gone through what I had. It did seem to be the strangest thing that my complexion was somehow more radiant since the transplant (not that I'm recommending it). Even some of the wrinkles and sagging skin seemed to have vanished. My eyes appeared to be bigger and brighter. Before my diagnosis, the inevitable signs of aging had, of course, become more and more apparent.

Like many women and some men, I had become very self-conscious about the changes that had come about with my aging. Before, when driving to work, which was just a few miles away, I would look at my reflection in the rear-view mirror at each and every one of the few stop signs along the way to check out not just the coloring of my make-up, comparing it to the lighting in the bathroom mirror where it had just been applied versus the outside light, but also to see if the wrinkles and sagging skin really looked as bad as I imagined. *Geez, like anything was really going to change from one stop sign to the next.* Still, I was obsessed.

One reason I was not utterly dumbfounded in feeling like my skin was better is the fact that when my mother was first diagnosed with multiple myeloma, they had her on the same drugs I was later put on when I was diagnosed. As Mom was 81, she naturally had signs of aging on her face, though she always did her best to camouflage them. I always thought her best cover-up was her beautiful smile. It is always difficult to see a parent age, and I couldn't help but notice those changes.

I so vividly remember being with her and a group of people at a restaurant one day, sometime after she started her treatments. The sun was shining on her face through the large windows there. As I watched her laughing and conversing with everyone, I thought she looked younger than she did before. How strange that seemed to me.

I have also heard of, but am not familiar with, anti-aging treatments using stem cells and/or a person's own blood. Who knows, but the compliments I was getting from other people were of a nature that would have been the answer to many of my prayers from the past. And just think, all I had to do to have those prayers answered was to cash in the cancer card I had never purchased, but that somehow ended up in my pocket, anyway. This card would stay with me for life—no refunds, returns, or exchanges.

Back to the lovely neighbors who reminded me at the end of every conversation they had with me to please let them know if there was anything they could do for Dave or me. One of the things that touched me the most was when just days after returning home from the hospital, the neighbor beside us, a friend and coworker of Dave's, called him on his cell phone somewhat early in the morning to ask him if I was sleeping. Dave told him no. This neighbor said he just needed to be sure, as he wanted to mow his lawn but would wait if I happened to be resting. How thoughtful was that?

Another day while Dave and I were out walking Smokey on the trails in our area, we passed a longtime friend who had also been one of Dave's coworkers. We chatted for a few minutes, and he asked how I was feeling. I told him I was doing okay. After our conversation ended and we walked on ahead a bit, he called out, "Is there anything, anything at all, I can do for you?"

I stopped dead in my tracks, overcome with emotions of gratitude, walked back to him, and hugged him tightly. "You just did the best thing anyone could ever do for me just by asking me that," I told him. That same person and his girlfriend also delivered a homemade meal to our home shortly after. It is heartwarming to know that people can be so thoughtful and caring. I did express my gratitude by delivering homemade chocolate chip cookies to them at their home soon afterward.

There were also some people who were members of a union Dave had once belonged to at work but had gotten out of sometime before, who were kind enough to contribute to our cause with a very generous check. They featured our story and picture in an edition of their union magazine. Many people in need who worked for the union or had a family member requiring assistance got help and also had their stories in this magazine.

Chapter Fifteen
Life on Cancer

Late one afternoon, while I was still at home on disability, I got a real surprise while I was in the house working on the computer. Dave was outside working on the lawn, and I heard him call my name, asking me to come out. A car unfamiliar to me was parked in front of the house, and Dave exclaimed, "Look who's is here to see you!"

The two occupants in the vehicle were a couple, Bob and Jeri, who were dear friends of ours but whom we had not seen in years. Jeri and I had worked together in the past. We had grown so close that she gifted me with a cruise ticket she purchased before becoming engaged to Bob, as she didn't want to leave home without him for a week. I also had the honor of being chosen to be one of their brides-maids when they married, and we are best of friends still. We are also part of each other's support system, as Bob has been fighting cancer for many years, and we can all relate so well to what each of us is going through.

So, when out of that car stepped Jeri, I was very pleasantly surprised. Not only had we not seen each other in years, I had no idea they were in the area. They had made a trip to town to see one of Bob's old friends and were on their way out when they decided to take a chance and swing by the house, hoping we may be home. Knowing my fragile condition, they did not come into the house or stay longer than a few minutes. Jeri and I talked on the front lawn, standing a few feet apart and posing for a picture together before they went on their way. I looked into the car as Bob sat waiting for us to complete our little visit and asked him how he was doing.

His cancer had been in remission for some time then. He was doing well and feeling optimistic about life. He wanted to share that sense of positivity with me and made mention of an experience he'd had during one of the many procedures he'd undergone. While doctors had tried removing a blockage from his throat, which had been caused by cancer, his heart had stopped for a few moments. His doctor was able to get it started again, but during those moments it was stopped, he'd had an out-of-body experience.

While I was more than anxious to hear his story, he didn't want to go into detail there in the car in front of the house, so he promised to tell me all about it over the phone whenever I was ready to listen. We said our goodbyes, and they headed home.

It did take me a while to prepare myself to make that phone call and ask Bob to share his story with me, though I was really anxious to hear it. After calling and speaking with Jeri for a while, I asked her if I could talk to him. He was more than up for the conversation, and she handed him the phone. For what was probably close to an hour, he went into detail about the experience he had when his heart stopped. Again, it was only for some short moments. Still, during that time, he has vivid memories of leaving his body and being in a space where family members he had lost in the past were present, standing and talking amongst themselves behind him. However, since it was not his time to go, they were not approaching him or even making themselves visible to him.

Who did make himself visible and speak to Bob was Jesus. The light surrounding Jesus center stage assured Bob that he was guiding him on his way, but He made it clear to him that it was not his time to go. Jesus told him his family still needed him and that he needed to go back.

Bob said being there with Jesus in spirit was such a comfortable feeling, and he had no fear. He then began hearing a voice and felt a force in contact with his physical being. This voice belonged to his doctor, who was shaking him, calling his name, urging him to come back. So, back he came, with a sense of peace and understanding that it was not his time to leave the life he had here.

I listened to his story in awe. Many people have reported experiences similar to this, and these stories intrigue me. I am a true believer in such things. As Bob finished his story, one of the most compelling things he said to me was, "Sandy, you're not going to die. It's not your time."

How I envied him for his confidence in making that statement. I would be afraid to tell someone that, especially with so much conviction, and especially to someone who has an incurable form of cancer. Still, I have to say, I believed in him when he said it, and I prayed to God to make it be true.

As I write this story, these two dear friends of mine are currently going through some extremely challenging times related to Bob's cancer, and we continue to be part of each other's support system.

One day before returning to work, I was tasked with making a trip to Santa Barbara to gather paperwork and information from the attorney handling my parents' estate. It would be the first time since returning home from the transplant that I would be driving somewhere out of town by myself. I was excited to get out of the house and embark on this little adventure. Though, I was a little apprehensive about driving into the city and looking for a business I'd never been to before. Not to mention the challenge of parking, as that's always an issue in the city.

Dave was even more concerned, and we printed out directions for me to have available in the car. I also needed to make the trip, take care of business and then make it back to town in time for a voice lesson I had scheduled for that day, which I was very excited about. Music is one of my favorite things, and I had taken voice lessons with a few different voice teachers in years past and really enjoyed them. I always fizzled out on them later, though, as work, family, and college courses took precedence, leaving me with little time or energy to pursue my own personal endeavors. Since I was home now and looking for ways to fill the time, this seemed the perfect antidote. I was beyond excited to get back into it.

That day was a good one for me all the way around. First, the beautiful drive into the city, locating the office building, finding parking without too much difficulty, and then making it home in time for my lesson gave me a slight sense of accomplishment at a time when I really needed it. After returning to work, I hung in with those voice lessons for a short period until life got in the way again, and I stopped going for quite some time.

It wasn't until about seven months after I begrudgingly retired that I reached out to that same music teacher and picked it up again.

It has become a joyous part of my life as I strive toward recovery. I continue this pursuit today, as well as writing lyrics for songs.

One day, I felt brave enough to tuck my pride beneath that thin gray scarf and blue baseball cap I wore to cover my bald head and venture out to our local Walmart. You were almost always guaranteed to run into people you knew there, whether you wanted to or not. Going there felt like an out-of-body experience, as I never thought I could or would have to go there like this. This was my life on cancer, though, and I knew I had to get used to living it. This wasn't my fault, and I knew I had to be mature enough to get over what people may think when they saw me like this.

One of the most memorable things I took away from that trip was when I passed through the store aisle where the container of loose DVDs was displayed. An elderly man stood beside it and fumbled with a handful of DVDs that had slipped from his fingers and scattered to the floor at his feet. His exasperated curses of frustration stopped abruptly when he looked over and saw me looking his way. He paused a moment and then asked, "How are you?"

I smiled back and said, "I'm fine, thanks. How are you?"

He smiled and nodded, seeming somewhat embarrassed at being so worked up over something so trivial compared to what I was currently facing at an age much younger than his. He nodded and smiled, his acknowledgment that he was fine too. He then said, "You're a brave lady."

I said, "Thank you; I appreciate that." I really did appreciate it, as he had no idea of the milestone he was witness to on that day.

As my shopping continued, I saw an employee who worked at the financial institution I worked at, but in a different department than mine. Still, we were pretty close. A big smile covered her face as she pulled me into her arms for an extended bear hug and a friendly kiss. I could see the tears glistening in her eyes as she said, "Love you, girl," and then continued on her way. I would meet up with another employee there that morning. He was the person who had mentored Tyler during his summer internship at the financial institution where we worked, and he, too, pulled me in for a big bear hug when he spotted me. What a help to my fragile sense of confidence it was during those moments they were kind enough to share with me.

One of the things I did accomplish during my months at home was going through a huge bag of poems I'd written years ago that I had stored in my closet. There were numerous rough drafts of my writings, along with some that were neatly printed, that I now took the time to separate and put in order. In addition, I gathered up other notebooks I had stashed in several other closets. Some had stories I had written as assignments in my junior high and high school English and composition classes. I'd gotten some pretty good grades on those papers. However, it was evident even then that I'd had a bad habit of procrastinating. There were almost always five points docked off the final scores of my papers because I had turned them in late.

Once I had everything in order, I spent hours typing those poems and stories on the computer. It made me feel like I had made valuable use of some of my time, along with the sense of accomplishment of completing something that had, in fact, been a distant goal in my mind for quite some time. Those poems and stories are now in alphabetical order and available for me to read anytime. There is one particular poem that I am aware of that went missing during that process. It was, in fact, in that bag somewhere when I got started, as I recall reading it, but it was nowhere to be found when I went to look for it. I remember some of it, though, and am hoping I can recreate it.

It seemed the time to go back to work would never come. While I remember the wait of those days, much of it is but a distant memory as four years have gone by now. There are so many times I wish I had kept a daily journal then. It's hard sometimes, though, to write when you're depressed, reminding yourself every day of a longing you have that no one can fulfill or make go faster. I do know my appetite returned, though it was often hard to eat as swallowing was still painful due to the damage to my throat made by the one chemo infusion. I regained my coffee cravings, which I satisfied once again perched on the love seat next to the window during my morning conversations with God. I continued with my daily walks and tried to stay positive.

I took advantage of any opportunity to take a drive with Dave anywhere, just to get out of the house and see some different scenery.

Chapter Sixteen
Back to Work

In September, my doctor released me to go back to work. She suggested starting back at more of a part-time pace rather than jumping back into full throttle. That, of course, never happened. Once I was there, I didn't want to leave.

I reported to the office bright and early on the morning of the 10th, my wig perfectly in place. I really was under the illusion that I could pick right back up on the working life I had left sitting there at my desk some five months before. There was also the illusion I could handle the supervisory position I'd taken on shortly before going out on disability. That was not, though, the way it turned out to be.

Along with the lack of self-confidence I had about being able to fulfill my duties in the new position I took before going out on leave, which was even more overwhelming now, and the trauma the treatment and transplant had taken on my body and brain, I was a mess. No amount of wishing for the old days when I felt like I knew what I was doing could bring that feeling back. The struggle to comprehend, process, and solve the simplest of things, those which had come so easily to me in the past after doing what I'd been doing for almost three decades, tore away at my already fragile sense of self-confidence and self-worth. Not only did I feel ignorant and incompetent, I assumed everyone around me saw me in the same light.

Along with the new duties of supervising (or at least trying to) came new computer programs I needed to learn, and you and I already know how computer illiterate I am. Still, I would knock myself out, trying to master them as best I could. There was one particular daily report I just couldn't get a handle on, no matter how hard I tried. I never did get the hang of it, and my boss, who worked so hard at being supportive and understanding of my situation, always had to take over that task, amongst many others. I would dwell on the negative thoughts I imagined he was having of me as he tried to oversee the department and my problems on top of it.

This same month, in fact, just a couple of weeks after my return to work, Dave went into the hospital to have major back surgery. He had been having issues with it for years, and it became evident that it was necessary to have the procedure done now rather than later to avoid permanent damage and his ability to walk normally. He had had a three-level fusion on his neck a little over a year before this time. His doctor had been delaying scheduling back surgery due to my situation. She was concerned about adding more stress to our household. She wanted to be sure I was physically and mentally able to handle the responsibility of caring for him afterward. We both assured her I was. I couldn't allow him to continue in his condition, and I was anxious to get this taken care of right away. So, bright and early on the day of his appointment, Dave and I drove to the hospital where the surgery would be performed, which is an hour south of us.

I sat by his bedside, as he had sat beside mine for numerous hours during my ordeal while they prepped him for the procedure. There were wires hooked up and taped all over his body. Having any operation on your back is scary, especially as there is always the chance of things being worse than they were before surgery if things are not done right. Even though we both had all the confidence in the world in this particular doctor, there was that apprehension, especially, of course, for Dave. This same doctor had also performed his neck surgery, which had turned out to be a godsend. The back surgery was also a huge success, and we felt that this woman, with her expert skills, was a lifesaver. This procedure, which was supposed to take four hours, ended up taking seven hours. He spent a couple more hours in the recovery room before I could go back to see him, and it was late by the time he was assigned to the room where he would spend the next few days.

Taking a day off work to get him to the hospital on the day of surgery, along with the time taken to go see him over the days he was in the hospital, was stressful for me, especially considering this was all taking place within the same month I had just returned to work. I felt terrible for having to take more time off. The day I went to pick him up to bring him home, I told my coworkers I was making the trip to Santa Barbara but that I'd do my best to be back before the end of the day.

One of the girls said, "Sandra, go be with your husband. He needs you."

I knew she was right and felt terrible that she was the one pointing this out and not me. How selfish could I be after all the sacrifices Dave had made while caring for me? During the first weeks of his recovery, I would take care of what I could before going to work in the morning and then come home every day for lunch to help him some more. I could make it there in just a few minutes, take off his bandages so he could shower and wash the incision site, and then bandage him back up when he was done. I would then help him put on his socks and shorts. From there, it was back to work. It was always a fight against time, and I added much more stress to the situation than was necessary.

To make matters worse, there was a nerve in Dave's arm that somehow had gotten tweaked, we believe, when his IV was taken out at the hospital, and it caused him terrible pain. He was a trooper, though, putting on his back brace and using a cane as he took a short walk around the block with me every night. We saw one of his coworkers on one of our walks one evening, and she dubbed us "The Golden Couple." I guess for getting through so many medical procedures (Dave had also had cataract surgery on both eyes recently) between us, and still going strong, even if slowly. Eventually, Dave found a gadget he could use to pick things up with and became less dependent on me for the little things I was doing for him.

I wanted to care for him as he had cared for me. I couldn't help thinking how nice it would have been if he could have been home on disability during the same time I had been, rather than right after I returned to work. Though I realize that may have been more difficult, it would have alleviated a lot of the guilt I felt for having such a strong desire to be at work, proving to myself and the rest of the world that I was capable of doing the job that I really was not capable of doing at all.

I wasn't ready to give up, though, and continued going to work every day, hoping that things would turn around for me. That I would regain the confidence and the more robust train of thought

I'd had before the transplant and all the chemo. Most days, my efforts were dismal. Dismal days led to sleepless nights, which, of course, made the situation that much worse. On the rare occasion that I did have a day when my thought process was somewhat better than expected, I would excitedly think, "My brains are back, my brains are back," only to find that the following day, I again had difficulty processing thoughts and information. It may have been easier on me had I not had those days when I thought things had returned to normal because, as the verse in one of my favorite Smokey Robinson songs goes, "A taste of honey is worse than none at all."

My struggles continued as time went on. I wanted so badly to feel like I was succeeding, not only in my position but also in helping those I was supposed to be supervising in theirs. To say I was failing at both was an understatement. Every issue, every phone call, every email or request from one of my bosses or coworkers blew into a major dilemma as I panicked about how to respond to each one. I felt far from useful to anyone. Those feelings carried on as we wrapped up 2018 with the usual festivities. It was so surreal to me to be wearing a wig to the parties we attended while wrapping up the year.

On a rainy weekend at the beginning of January 2019, a bunch of family members and numerous friends celebrated one of our nieces' birthdays in an area out of town. A group of buildings clustered within walking distance of each other served wine, beer, and other spirits that we visited. Despite the cold and rain on the walks, we all enjoyed ourselves. A group of us met for dinner before retiring to our hotel rooms that night and for breakfast the following day before heading home.

Life was good. I felt healthy, loved, and thankful to be out and about on this little adventure. Within days, however, I developed a cough that lingered longer than expected. This was winter, though, and some of the others in my office had coughs and sniffles too. So, as usual, I didn't take my situation too seriously. Remember, I got over my ailments almost immediately in my life BC.

As time passed, the cough worsened, and Dave finally convinced me to make a doctor's appointment. My primary physician was not on duty the day I called in, so I went in to see the attending doctor on duty. After examining me, he, too, did not feel like it was anything more than a common cold and sent me home with the usual advice of drinking lots of fluids and getting lots of rest. I returned to work and my hectic schedule.

My chest continued getting more congested, though, and the coughing worsened. Soon, I was stopping to bend over during the coughing fits I was having when walking through the halls of my office building, trying to catch my breath. I again called my primary physician's office, and this time was able to get in and see him. He agreed I had something more than a mild cold going on and put me on a mild antibiotic.

I was grateful to fill that prescription, though things got held up at the pharmacy when I got there. It seemed nothing could go smoothly for me. Still, I did my best to stay positive. Even with the antibiotics, though, my symptoms grew worse. I went back again to see my doctor, who, by this time, diagnosed me with bronchitis and put me on a more potent antibiotic. I filled that prescription and followed it to a T. My condition grew worse still.

I was obsessed with trying to go to work and downplay my illness. As I so often did, I was trying to prove to myself and the rest of the world that I was some kind of superhero. Why, why, why was I doing this? Why does anyone do this kind of thing to themselves? Ego is my only guess. A driving desire to feel needed and essential.

That second round of antibiotics was not doing much better, and I sunk further still.

At this point, I was at least surrendering to the fact that I needed to stay home from work. After all, wasn't that me who had always felt that it was selfish of people who knowingly came into work sick? Who was willing to sacrifice the health of others for their own sake? Now, to satisfy my drive to accomplish my work goals and prove I really wanted to be there, I was becoming one of those people. There, too, was the fear of falling even further behind in my job and my new position since so much time had already been lost while I'd been out on disability with the transplant. The coughing became horrendous, and soon my whole body, particularly my back, ached from the constant pressure I was putting on it as I tried to catch my breath.

There had been a couple of instances before when I had pulled my back, leaving me laid up and miserable for a week or more. I'd also taken a fall off my niece Cassandra's very tall thoroughbred mare years before, leaving me injured and on crutches for about six weeks.

One day, when I was so sick, Tyler drove me to an appointment with a local chiropractor that Dave had made for me. This person was also a good friend of ours. He adjusted my back, which helped me feel somewhat better.

Thankful for any relief, back home we went, where I tried to get more rest. It didn't help. The congestion worsened, the cough was almost constant, and my frustration grew.

Chapter Seventeen
Collapsed Vertebrae

One morning, I was determined to go to work no matter what. I let Dave know of my intentions, and I heard him sarcastically tell Tyler, "Yeah, your mother thinks she's going to go to work."

While trying to get out of bed, it became apparent it was something I would not be able to accomplish by myself, so I called Dave into the back room for help. He grabbed my arm and attempted to pull me up. Then, as I tried to twist, roll over, and lift my legs up and off the bed, I felt a horrendous pain in my lower back.

Though we didn't know it then, we would later learn that I had a herniated disk between my 4th and 5th lumbar. I believe it may have been at that moment that my vertebrae collapsed.

The pain was horrible. I never made it to work that day. I believe it was this same day that Dave packed me up in the car and took me to the emergency room in a small town about fifteen miles from us, where we knew there would be a shorter wait time than if we went to our local ER. There, we explained my situation, and though doctors scanned my back, they found nothing wrong. They were kind enough to hook me up to an IV long enough to give me some intravenous painkillers, which gave me some temporary relief, and prescribed some oral pain medication for me to pick up from the pharmacy.

Even on the meds, the pain was unbearable. The following day, Dave packed me up in the car. He drove me fifty miles south to the emergency room of yet another hospital, hoping for better answers. En route, he called and left a message with the frontline staff at my primary physician's office, requesting a call back from my doctor as soon as possible. Thankfully, we soon heard back from him, and Dave explained the situation. He wanted some validation that he was making the best decision.

My doctor assured him that he was. Once in the emergency room, it again seemed like we waited forever. I bounced one knee continuously, trading between the two, trying desperately to keep my mind off the pain. Finally, I was evaluated and put into a room to dress in a hospital gown to scan my back. This one was more sophisticated than the one I'd had done the day before.

I remember getting up off the bed to head to the sink when I felt another coughing fit coming on. The amount of green and yellow crud that had been coming up and out of my lungs lately had been beyond my belief, and I wanted to be able to spit it out. I looked at the nurse standing nearby and told her she might want to look away, as this would not be pretty. Then, kind of laughing, I said, "I don't know what I'm talking about; I'm sure you see much worse than this on a daily basis."

After the scan was done and after heeding my pleas for relief from my pain, I was hooked up to an IV and given pain medication intravenously. When the lower-level painkillers proved to have little to no effect, the doctor bumped it up to morphine. I thanked God for the temporary relief.

I was eventually admitted to the hospital for an overnight evaluation, and Dave drove home for some rest. He returned in the morning; I was discharged, and back home we went. Our plan was to seek advice from the doctor who had done Dave's back surgery. When we left, we didn't realize that the bag of pain medication we'd taken to the hospital to show the doctors what I was on had been left behind with the front office, and now I had none.

We had the choice of making another hundred-mile round trip back down south to pick it up or trying to have the newly filled prescription immediately refilled at our local pharmacy. That's not easy to get by insurance companies, which will only pay for meds in specific time intervals. I can't recall how we did it, but we acquired more pain meds. I returned to my backroom sanctuary, trying to heal and not be more of a burden to Dave than I already had been for the past two years.

The coughing kept up at a relentless pace, and I tried to stay ahead of the pain. Never, EVER in my life, have I been so sick. My goal was to lay as still as possible, as moving seemed to spark the urge to cough, which caused more pressure on my back. There is a nightstand at the side of our bed with square corners, and I would grab onto it when I felt the urge to cough, to try to steady my body, lessening the jarring of my back. Eventually, the palm of my right hand became sore due to my continuous death grip on the corner of that nightstand.

A wastebasket was next to that nightstand that was always full of soiled Kleenex. I was constantly coughing and blowing my nose.

Soon, Dave got me in to see his back doctor. After reviewing the results of my X-rays taken at the hospital down south, she determined that I was not a candidate for the type of surgery she performed and referred me to one of her colleagues. An appointment was made to see him, but it would be a wait, and the time in between was hell. The pain was constant, and I kept up with a steady intake of painkillers. These medications tend to cause constipation, which became yet another source of misery to be added to my already sorry state. Trying to go through the motions of getting things moving in that respect, of course, required putting pressure on my lower back, causing more pain, which naturally led to me not wanting to try to go at all. This caused a decrease in my appetite and my desire to eat, resulting in more weight loss.

Life seemed almost unbearable during this time, not just for me, of course, but for Dave and Tyler, too. I was either sitting in the recliner in our family room on a heating pad or lying in bed in the back room, trying to rest without moving, so I could heal. The congestion and the pressure in my lungs were such that I was honestly scared to fall asleep at night for fear of choking to death in my sleep. A worry my doctor later assured me would not have happened.

Still, not knowing that at the time, my concerns led to my trying to fall asleep on a pillow in a slightly upright position. Dave slept in another room in a desperate attempt to give me some quiet space and get some rest himself. The added stress of what my health was once again putting on him made this difficult situation even worse for me.

The day finally came for us to drive south, to see the doctor referred to us by Dave's surgeon. Dave drove the fifty miles south while I once again bounced my knee along the way, switching between the two and periodically holding my breath. Just as we headed out, my sister Jeanette called my cell phone, explaining that our sister Barbara's health was in grave condition. She did not, though, want our trip to my appointment interrupted.

Once at the doctor's office, we signed in, and Dave sat down. I paced the floor of the waiting room in an effort to alleviate some of the pain and keep my mind distracted. We were called back to a room to see the doctor, who had the X-rays of my spine up against a light for us to see. While I paced that room, he and Dave examined and discussed the images. This doctor suggested I have a procedure called a "kyphoplasty." I was actually familiar with this term, as it was the same option a doctor had recommended my mother have done after the car accident she'd been involved in left her with an injured back. She never did go through with it, as her pain had eventually subsided. I remember how odd I thought this type of thing had sounded when she explained it to me.

This minor surgery entails a doctor inserting a needle through the skin and muscle of your backbone, inflating a balloon into the collapsed vertebra, and then filling that area with cement. How strange that just a year from the time it was suggested as a treatment for my mother, it was now being offered as the best resort for me in my situation. No matter how odd it sounded, I wanted it done as soon as possible—anything to alleviate this miserable pain. Unfortunately, there would be a wait time, and I couldn't imagine how I would survive it. Back home, I again dined on pain medication and tried to be as still as possible.

One of the days during that period, my manager from work called me and told me that our group had put together a little care package for me and that she wanted to deliver it to the house. I had on my little gray headscarf and the blue baseball cap when the knock came at the door. Dressed in my gray leggings, which really accentuated my emaciated body, I opened my front door to find her and the employee who had cried in my arms the day my story came out in the paper, standing there with excited smiles. They held a basket of healing gifts in their hands, which included a nice cozy blanket that I cuddle with to this day.

I smiled, so excited to see them there. I started to try to ask them in. Still, as soon as I drew in a breath to talk, I went into such a violent coughing fit I had to step back from the door into the house, bend over and hold on to the corner of the kitchen counter. At the same time, I fought to clear my chest and catch my breath. The fit did not pass quickly. My coworkers did not come in. They said they did not want to interrupt my rest and left.

Around this time, I reached out to my primary care doctor again, asking for a stronger antibiotic for my bronchitis. A third round was prescribed, and Dave picked it up from the pharmacy. All the while, my sister Barbara's health was getting worse. I could do nothing but worry about her condition. At the same time, Jeanette continued to try to care for her while working her own full-time job and taking care of her family.

Jeanette's tearful call came late one afternoon, the last week in January 2019. She informed me that the nurse at the hospital had called and told her that Barbara was once again in the hospital and, more than likely, wouldn't make it this time. Though we had known to expect this call for some time now with her COPD and other health issues, we were, of course, still horrified. No matter my condition, I knew I needed to make it to the hospital. Jeanette and her husband came by my house to collect me, and we drove into town to pick up our brother.

Standing at the side of Barbara's hospital bed in my mask, we held her hands. We listened as her doctor came in and asked her if she wanted all measures taken to sustain her life or if the effort should simply be to keep her as comfortable as possible while the inevitable unfolded. Barbara was a regular there with her health issues, and he was more than familiar with her case. His voice had no kindness or emotion when he addressed her with these options. I had a déjà vu moment from when the doctor first approached my father's bedside after he was brought into this same hospital after a bleeding stroke in his brain. He had been asked these same questions in the same matter-of-fact fashion. I get that medical staff must be tough to remain in this field; still, these things are hard on patients and difficult for family members to witness.

Barbara's answer was almost comical to me when she came back with a jolly, "Well, I don't want to try and live forever and ever, but I'd like to try and stay alive today."

She was eventually taken from the room in the emergency area to a private room, where nurses gathered around her, administering their best efforts to save her life. We siblings, as well as two of the part-time home caregivers whose care she had been under for some time, gathered around her bedside, encouraging her in her fight to breathe and survive. She became fitful in her struggle, her entire being thrashing about as breathing became more difficult. She started asking us to leave the room. We, of course, could not bring ourselves to go. We simply kept telling her how much we loved her and wanted her to stay with us. She finally became insistent that we all leave.

I remember trying to take the jewelry off her fingers, knowing that things sometimes can disappear in these situations. My attempts were futile, though, as her fits were now almost violent, and her fingers were too swollen for anything to slide off of them without her cooperation. It would have to wait. We stayed by her bedside as long as we could until her requests that we leave turned somewhat vicious. "I love you, Barbara," I cried

"I love you too," she responded, "now get out." Those were the last words she said to us. We honored her request and left her there with her wish to die with dignity. How the memory of our final moments together, laced with those words, hurts.

We left the hospital, knowing she might not make it through the night. Surprisingly she did. The following morning Jeanette called me to say the nurse checked in with her and that it would be a good idea for us to come to see Barbara as soon as possible, as she wouldn't have long. Very few minutes passed before Jeanette called me back in tears, saying she had just gotten another call from the nurse informing her that Barbara was already gone.

The Old Red Barn and my grandparent's motel as it looked when I was a child.

My first time in the saddle on Shay.

My in-laws Tom and Barbara Pickles showing support in the shirts made up for my cause.

Railey sporting her support.

Chapter Eighteen

Kyphoplasty

Jeanette told me her husband, Corky, would come by in an hour to pick me up and bring me to their house so I could ride with her to the hospital. I said, "Okay," trying not to break down while I was still on the phone with her. Our conversation ended, and I sat on my bed, blinded by tears, and hit the disconnect button on my cell phone twice, trying to end our call quickly. I did not want her to hear the howls that were making their way up through my throat.

I sat there awhile after the call ended, screaming my tears of loss and frustration aloud. Waves of intense pain shattered me physically and emotionally as I shook my head and body, trying to throw the sensations aside. I knew I had to get in the shower and get dressed so I would be ready by the time my ride got there. The strange thing was that Jeanette's husband knocked on my door fifteen minutes after our phone call had ended. He came in, gave me a big hug, and told me to take all the time I needed to get ready.

I would later learn that I had, in fact, not adequately ended that phone call, leaving Jeanette to listen to my screams and prompting her to send Corky over right away.

We got to the hospital and entered the room where my niece was kneeling at the bedside of Barbara's lifeless body. Her eyes were still open.

We cried while doing our best to console each other. Grief turned into frustration when we later asked the staff for the rings and other jewelry that had been on Barbara's body when she passed. It didn't seem anyone could account for those items. After spending a very long time going through that room, finding an earring or two that she may have yanked off in her distress, one of the employees came into the room with the wedding ring we were most concerned about and said, "Oh well, this was found on the floor a little while ago. Is this it?"

My niece grabbed it from her hand and said, "Yes, now where's the other one?"

Some of those other items were never accounted for, and we had to let the situation go. Our family was just dealing with too many things, and we had to pick our battles. I was too stressed out to focus on anything. My brain was nothing but a big blur, making it nearly impossible to function mentally at all.

Now we were was dealing with losing another sister, just ten months after losing our mother, who we'd lost just ten months after losing our father.

There is still, of course, cancer, the back injury, the anticipation of surgery, and the stress of a lawsuit filed against my mother's insurance company by those persons riding in the car my mother hit while driving in town two days after our father's passing, losing time from work yet again, the complications of sorting through our parents' estate and now, how to help Jeanette deal with Barbara's estate, which she had been named executor of. There were other issues on top of these, too numerous to mention.

Barbara passed February 1st, 2019. On February 6th, I went in for the kyphoplasty that I prayed would relieve the pain and help heal my collapsed vertebra. Quite honestly, by this time, the pain had somewhat diminished. I might have recovered without this procedure like my mother had, though I was told my spine may not have healed straight if I did not go through with it. The doctor said the surgery would be pretty simple and should only take an hour or so. I couldn't get started with it fast enough.

I sat with the front of my body pressed against the chair designed for this type of thing, and my hospital gown opened up in the back. It's funny that one of the things I remember most about it was how embarrassed I was that the handsome young man assisting the doctor, who couldn't have been much older than my son, had to see my bare backside and my oversized purple cotton underwear.

The young lady who had helped prepare me that morning had asked me if I had any questions or concerns about the procedure. I asked her how long I would have to wait before riding a horse after this procedure. It wasn't that I had a horse to ride, but riding was one of the things I was hoping to do again soon as a way to start healing my heart from everything that had been going wrong in my life. She went to ask the doctor, returned to the room, and told me at least three months. Good to know.

Another of the great advantages of having this surgery was that since the doctor would be going inside my backbone, he could gather a bone marrow sample for my oncologist to examine without my having to go through another bone marrow biopsy. How convenient was that!? So, with the procedure complete and my required recovery time in the doctor's office served, Dave drove me home, and I began the healing process.

There was a bandage on my back covering the incision, which was sore, and I had to move slowly when lying down or preparing to sit. Dave again played nursemaid, caring for me, changing out the bandage when necessary, and bringing me whatever I needed while sitting.

Other family members did their best to be supportive, too. I had made an appointment with my sister-in-law, Jill, to have a pedicure before I got so sick. Rather than have me cancel it, since I couldn't go to the salon, she brought her foot tub and supplies to the house. She did my pedicure in our living room while I lounged in the recliner. How spoiled was I?

Another sister-in-law, Angela, offered to bring in lunch from the restaurant of my choice and stay for a visit one day. I chose my favorite meal from our local Thai restaurant, ordering it medium-spicy as I always did. Guess I should have known better, as the spices hitting my raw throat resulted in me having coughing fits, leaving me unable to talk much during our visit. Still, the food was so good, and it was wonderful to have company. Our niece, Madison, recommended that I be recognized and celebrated as a cancer survivor at a special event being held at her high school for local cancer victims. The list of honorees included those who were fighting cancer as well as the families of those who had sadly succumbed to it. A number of family members joined in support at that event.

Again, there does come a day, though you can't believe it in the moments of your misery, that you start to feel better. When the pain and soreness slowly become a dull ache, and you think that you might actually feel like your old self one day. That day came, and I was finally able to return to work. I clearly recall the first morning I was back at my desk, and my manager approached me when he arrived at the office. I looked up at him, and he asked how I was feeling.

I shook my head and said, "I can't do that again." I told him that this last experience was worse than the cancer and what I went through with my transplant. I said I could not continue trying to live like I was some kind of superhero who could conquer all when I should already have known this was not and would never be the case.

He was so sympathetic, trying to encourage me to continue fighting. He told me that when his mother experienced challenging times, she knew it was the devil at work, but she also knew those tough times would pass through faith and prayer.

Later that month, Dave and I went to my regularly scheduled monthly appointment with my oncologist. He told us he had studied the bone marrow sample provided to him by my back doctor and was pleased to report he didn't see any cancer markers showing up. This was great news. My back was feeling better, I was back at work, my cancer was under control, and life was good. That is until it wasn't.

The following month, Dave and I showed up for my regular doctor's appointment with no reason to be anxious about anything he might have to say. Especially with the great news we'd gotten last month on the results from the study of the bone marrow extracted from my back the month before. So, we were not prepared for what came next. I cannot recall the exact words my doctor used to inform us that those damn markers did, in fact, show up in my blood tests this month, which meant the cancer was, in fact, active again. I do, however, remember the words I wanted to say but didn't (at least I hope I didn't): "Are you f**king kidding me??"

Again, it seems there does come a time when you get desensitized to the sucker punches that keep coming your way. I had learned some time before this moment to take a deep breath, or in some cases no breath at all, and blow them off as they came at me. There had been so damn many of them over the past few years that I was beginning to resign myself to the fact that sometimes it was better just to stay lying on the ground rather than try to get up. Especially since there was a good chance I would be going down again soon. This punch, though, took my breath away and caused time to stop. My life, from the moment of diagnosis until this moment when we sat listening to the words coming out of my doctor's mouth, flashed before my eyes. Every heartbreaking detail. Not just my heartbreak, mind you, but all those hearts that had been broken along the way with mine during this journey.

It had only been ten, maybe eleven, months since the transplant, and four or five of them had been spent at home healing. How could this be? My doctor did, though, have a wonderful way of smoothing over rough news and touchy situations. He spoke gently, assuring us that these things happen, that it was nothing I did or didn't do, and that there was no explanation as to why it had come back so quickly. He spoke with a tone of confidence that carried over to us that said, "Hey, this is no big deal. I've already got a plan lined up for us, and by the way, you've got this."

In my mind, something must not have gone right with the transplant, and I wanted to grill my doctor up north for answers. For God's sake, I hadn't even made it to my yearly checkup, which was, in fact, scheduled and on the calendar for May.

The doctor went on to explain to Dave and me that the next course of action would now be immunotherapy, along with the identical oral chemo capsules I had been taking before the transplant. These immunotherapy treatments were one and the same as those my mother had been put on when her numbers had gone up. The ones that caused her to feel like she was going to die, sending her into that panic attack that pushed her into a night's stay in the hospital.

My schedule would be treatments once a week for eight weeks, then every other week for another eight treatments (totaling sixteen weeks). After that, I would go for treatment once a month. These infusions lasted between five and six hours, so with the trips there and home, it would be an all-day thing.

That evening Jeanette called to check in on me and ask how my appointment went. I explained to her cancer had shown back up and that I would now have to have infusions.

She said, "Sandra, just promise me you won't go on the treatments that put Mom in the hospital."

I already knew they were one in the same. For all my life, I would have promised anything in the world to her; but I responded, "Jeanette, if that is what my doctor recommends for me to do to fight this cancer, that's what I have to do." What choice did I have if I wanted to live? Which I wholeheartedly did.

I explained to her that I did want to have a conversation with my doctor up north, explain this turn of events, and at least get her opinion on what may have gone wrong. Though I knew it was unreasonable on my part to expect her to know or have any more explanation than my local oncologist did, I still needed to try to get some answer as to why, after all the hell Dave and I had gone through with that process, the cancer had come back so quickly. I also figured that since my local doctor had already discovered the return of this beast and already had a plan in place for me, there really was no need to go back up north for my yearly checkup. We might as well save ourselves the five to six-hundred-mile round trip, and the time off work we would both have needed to take to make it there.

I put in a call to the doctor's office to cancel my appointment, with the hope that I could speak with her at the same time. I only got as far as communicating with her assistant. I explained the situation to her and asked that she have the doctor call me. She was so sorry to hear about this turn of events and assured me that she would pass my request on to the doctor to return my call. I am still waiting for that call.

Chapter Nineteen

Someone Went and Told the Devil

When it comes to having cancer, it would be more than a self-ish thought or question on my part if I were ever to have the audacity to ask, "Why me?" Especially since so many people in this world have cancer, and many more will be diagnosed with it in the future.

What I do feel justified in asking is why all five of my parents' children have been struck down in some way, shape, or form. Their firstborn, a daughter, the least serious, had to have a kidney removed due to it being cancerous. Their second born, another daughter, losing her life in a car accident at the tender age of seventeen. Their third child, their only son, struck down at nineteen with mental illness during his first semester in college and suffering from it still today. Their fourth born, a daughter, losing her life at 60 due to poor health conditions, and me, their fifth child, being diagnosed with a fatal form of cancer at age 57.

During the time we had spent in waiting rooms at the hospital up north, Dave and I seemed to quite often spot a particular young man who wore a baseball cap with the words "F**k Cancer" on it.

I could not have known then how all-consuming that emotion would become for me in the years to come or the anger that would develop between myself and this disease that I refer to and picture as the devil.

In the same way, I draw into the well of optimism my mother left behind for me in order to stay positive; I draw from that well of anger down deep in my soul that the devil and this disease have embedded there when I need fighting power.

After learning the cancer was back, I grew even more angry at life, and the devil, who I figured was to blame for all this. Going into somewhat of a mental rage, I beckoned him to stand before me so I could look him in the eye while I screamed in his face, "F**king bring it."

God had been covering for me long enough, though, and I probably should have known better than to tempt fate. Especially in light of everything the devil had already managed to put my family and me through. Still, I was determined that the devil would not have my soul in life or in death, and I trusted in God to be sure of that. It felt so damn good to lash out with this unfamiliar anger that even I didn't know I was capable of feeling.

There was a conversation I had with a friend who gathered with us at our family's Easter celebration the month after we learned about the return of this beast. She inquired as to how my health was doing. I explained the recent chain of events to her, getting so worked up that I told her about my words and gestures toward the devil and his evil. She said she could certainly understand my feeling this way and promised to pray for me.

I later channeled that anger into a deeper sense of determination in my decision to not allow the devil to take over my body, my brain, or my life, and to seal that deal with myself, I again put pencil to paper to still the conflicts raging inside me, the determination to come to grips with my situation, and my desire to keep moving forward. It resulted in my writing this poem.

"Someone Went and Told the Devil"

Someone went and told the devil how much I love to dance,
So when he saw a stumble in my step, he thought he saw his chance.

A chance to take down someone strong,
Never mind that his intentions were wrong.

He led me through a dance he designed to take me down,
It never once occurred to him that I might just stand my ground.

The music started playing as my father slipped away,
The devil and this dance were the reason he couldn't stay.

Still, stay he did long enough to be sure that I would see,
Just how strong the man was who made me and, in turn, taught me to be.

The devil then gave to me the same disease he'd given to my mother,
He cast her soul into the shadows, and through this dance, I lost another.

On to hell, we danced along while I fought off this disease,
And when he saw my step was stronger, he came and brought it back to me.

But instead of stopping there, he continued his attack,
And to return my step into a stumble, he went on to break my back.

The devil then chose a tune for me familiar from my past,
To distract me from the cries of my sister as she passed.

The only mercy he ever showed me was keeping from my dad,
The presence of the deadly disease his youngest child has.

It's amazing to me what one heart can survive,
And continue to beat beyond the events it needs to, just to stay alive.

Even I didn't know then the strength that I had,
'Til a fire burned inside my soul once that devil really made me mad.

Oh, how clever it was of him to hide the horror in a song,
Knowing that when the music started, I would dance along.

Well, music is my friend, and it won't do me wrong,
I will always find salvation embraced within a song.

Good will always overtake evil; just you wait and see,
Is all I have to say to that someone who went and told the devil on me.

Sandra R. Pickles

September 6, 2020

So, on top of all the stress I am already under at work, there is now the extra added stress of breaking this new news to my management team and explaining the new treatment regimen I would now be under, which would, of course, require, yet again, more time off. This just after the numerous weeks I had been out with my back and bronchitis.

Still, it had to be done. All managers were again supportive and understanding, insisting I take all the time I needed to focus on my health.

The time arrived for my first treatment. My doctor had me scheduled under a two-day window in case I had an adverse reaction to the drug and had to receive half of it one day and the other half the next. I, of course, was already familiar with this drill, knowing of my mother's experience. Since I felt like I usually held up pretty well under such circumstances, I wasn't concerned about a bad reaction. You can imagine then how disappointed I was in myself when shortly after being hooked up to the IV, and the drug started dripping through, I had to admit to the nurses that I was having difficulty breathing. They immediately jumped to slow down the drip time of the drug to counteract its effects and my reaction. Soon after, my lungs relaxed, the tightening sensation faded, my breathing slowed, and returned to normal.

Wow, that was an unpleasant experience. I understood now why my mother had panicked. It's a horrible sensation when you feel like you can't get enough air in your lungs to control your breathing.

The following day, I returned to receive the second half of that first dose and don't recall having an issue. I was required to stay for a specific time after the drug was administered to ensure I would not have any adverse reactions. I didn't.

So, on went those weekly, day-long treatments for eight weeks. There were no more bad reactions, and as I had had to do for quite some time now, I accepted and settled into a routine required of me to fight this battle. The hardest thing for me to try to control was the stress of having to miss so much work when I was already so anxious in trying to stay afloat, even when I was there. Again, in my troubled mind, every issue that came up was an extreme emergency. If I couldn't resolve it at that moment, it became one more thread in the rope tightening around my throat. Almost all tasks assigned to me in my new position as supervisor became impossible endeavors that I made much more complex than they had to be.

One thing I struggled most with was organization, prioritizing the things I needed to get done while trying to be present for the unexpected things that come one's way in the ordinary course of a workday.

One gal I went through my management program with worked in a nearby office and was very proficient in these areas. She offered to spend time with me every week to try to help me better perfect those practices. It was so kind of her to give up some of her time when she was also swamped. She even offered to sign up for an Excel class with me, knowing my struggles with computer programs. How sweet was that? While the Excel class never took place, I not only learned so much from her in the time she took me in at her busy desk, I grew more confident knowing I mattered to her as a person, friend, and professional.

On May 22nd, 2019, one day after the first anniversary of my transplant, and long after Dave had been trying to convince me to lose the wig I kept hiding under, I decided I was ready to show the world my first short hairdo. It was a long time in coming, and I had been telling Dave during the times he tried to convince me I looked fine without it that he had to let me be ready to take this step. Let me tell you, though, when this morning did come, I couldn't shed that wig fast enough.

In fact, I was so excited that I stood in the kitchen and posed for a selfie. I had taped a postcard in the background that showed a baby on his belly, looking like he was trying to fly. The caption under it made a reference to believing in yourself, which I thought was quite fitting. I then sent that picture out in a group text to Dave, friends, and family members, and in it, I said, "First day going to work without my wig. What do you think?"

They all, of course, responded with words of admiration for my new look, some saying how cute and sassy it looked. I responded with thanks, confirming that I really needed to hear this since it was way past time for me to put my big girl panties on and get on with life. That elated feeling followed me throughout the day. Not only did I go to work feeling like a brave new person who didn't mind showing the world my natural hair, but I also found myself looking for a reason to bounce through the halls of the different departments in my building to see how many people noticed I was wig free and au naturel. Most of those people were pleasantly surprised to see me like this and complimented my hairstyle. For those who didn't, I would ask, "So, how do you like my hair??"

By the time I got through those eight weeks of treatments and started going every other week, I had a routine going. I sent out regular reminders via email to everyone in my department, wrote on our department whiteboard the days I would be out, and had a good habit of setting up my out-of-office email for those days and recording my days of absence on my voicemail greeting.

Since my days in that chair started around 9 a.m. and ended at 3 or 4 p.m., I made big lunches that usually consisted of a tuna fish sandwich on toast, bags of fruits, vegetables, and a container of milk. How I looked forward to those sandwiches and would usually chow down on them way before noon! I now refer to these days in the cancer center as my healing days. I was away from my desk, away from the gnawing feeling of inadequacy, and I knew that no one would be expecting anything out of me while I was hooked up to an IV all day.

I would read, daydream, chat with the friendly nurses, and sometimes nap when the Benadryl they gave me as part of my premeds got the best of me. I don't know why I initially tried to conquer that weariness, trying to work through it and stay awake. I can still hear the voice of one of the nurses saying to someone as she walked through the infusion room that she didn't know why patients fought it when they felt the need to sleep. While I was the worst offender of that very thing, I had no answer either. Why does our society and our egos teach us that it is a badge of honor to wear proudly if we are able to get by and perform at lightning speed in our lives on little to no sleep? I have learned, a bit begrudgingly, not only that it doesn't work that way, but just how detrimental it is to our health, both mentally and physically.

In the days when Tyler was a baby, and I went back to work after my maternity leave was up, I got very little sleep. The few hours I did get were broken at best. When one of the young ladies who worked in my area asked how I got through the day with so little rest, I looked at her and said, "Adrenaline and lots of coffee!" What else was there??

One day when I showed up for treatment, I was told my blood counts were too low to undergo the infusions. *What??* I was up and ready for the day, made the trip here, and now you're telling me I can't have the treatment I came for? Well, since I'm up, dressed, and ready for the day, I might as well go to work.

I went in, and my boss, surprised to see me, called me into her office. We sat behind closed doors while I explained the morning's events. I then went into my office and put in a day's work.

Another time I went in for my infusion, I was told there was an issue with my insurance company authorizing my treatment, and I may have to miss this one too. "Oh, hell no," was my response upon hearing this. Treatment was my plan for the day. Dave and I had made the trip here, and I wanted my infusion, damn it! And anyway, I had my tuna fish sandwich packed up, along with the reading materials I was looking forward to enjoying that day, and I wasn't going to miss out. Fortunately, one of the nurses was able to contact the insurance company regarding the hold-up and get authorization for my treatment. Things ended up going on as scheduled. I was so appreciative of her willingness to go above and beyond.

Chapter Twenty
Sacrifices

One day while getting my infusion, I sat next to a young lady who was also getting treatment. I guessed that she was in her early to mid-thirties. She had long blonde hair, and her face seemed full of healthy color. She was accompanied by a gentleman, who I assumed was her husband, and an older woman, who I believe may have been her mother-in-law. They were discussing their kids' schedules, which one was where, and when they needed to be picked up. Not that I was trying to listen, mind you, I try to respect people's privacy as much as I like mine respected. Still, there was little distance between the chairs we occupied, and one couldn't help but hear conversations going on around them there.

The older woman got up to leave, on her way to pick up one of the kids from the sounds of it. I turned my head in the other direction and closed my eyes for a few moments. When I turned back around, I found this young couple in a tight embrace. He stood, reaching down to her, and she sat with her arms reaching up to him and around his neck. I immediately turned my head back to look in the other direction, not only out of respect for their privacy during that very personal moment, but also because I was so overwhelmed with emotion.

I could feel the desperation in their embrace, and hear their unspoken plea to God, as they begged for the miracle they would need to fight this battle and keep their family whole. My throat squeezed tight in the way it does when it is warning you that you're about to cry. A heaviness descended on my chest as I tried to pull it together and not allow my tears to fall. This was a young family with children who would need their mother and a husband who needed his wife. "Why, why," I asked myself, "could I cry for these people I had never seen before and would probably never see again (and I haven't) when I couldn't shed a tear for myself in my own situation?"

Another day, I remember sitting in the waiting room to see the doctor and noticing one of the magazines on the table had an article about multiple myeloma. Hoping to learn more about this disease that now seemed to be the center of my life, I read it. It was interesting, and I did learn a few things. The only line in it that I can quote to this day is the one the article ended with: "The one thing certain about this disease is that it is always fatal." Wow. Not sure if I was the author of that piece, I would have ended it (no pun intended) that way.

How many experiences did I have to have, and how much knowledge did I have to gain in a subject I had never wanted to know anything about in the first place? This was definitely not the subject of any of the college courses I had stood in line to sign up for.

Treatments eventually slowed to once a month, and I was able to spend more time at work. Not that it improved my performance.

174

In fact, in some ways, it made it worse. There was more time now to sit at my desk and feel inadequate in the work world, not just in front of myself, but in front of everyone else in the office. There was a constant sense in my gut that I was sinking. Still, I didn't want to give up.

The day did come, though, that I had to accept the fact that my incompetence was hindering the department I was trying to supervise. I wasn't doing anybody any good, least of all myself, and I was tired of feeling like a failure.

The sting of reality settled in the day I gave in and suggested to my manager that it might be better for everyone if I stepped back from my coveted position of collections supervisor to my previous role of collections officer. He immediately agreed. I didn't blame him. It had to be such a relief to him.

For the rest of the world, that moment wasn't even a notice in time. For me, it was a moment of eternity. The eternity it had taken me to get into this seat I had just been sitting in, the eternity I was now facing, knowing what I was offering to give up. Something I hadn't had for but a minute and would probably never have again. Now I had to turn my back on it because of what cancer had brought into my life.

My college experience and work career flashed before my eyes in quite the same way my cancer life had flashed before my eyes after learning of its return after the transplant. It wasn't just those days when I was single, mind you, holding down two jobs while trying to work in college courses. It was also those days after being married, having a baby, and trying to be a wife, mother, full-time employee, and part-time student. These sacrifices were not only mine. They were Dave's and Tyler's too.

175

I was constantly rushing from one task to another, running off to classes, and stressing out about homework while feeling guilty about neglecting our child. There were so many times I felt ashamed of myself for putting the success of my college and work career before that of being home with him.

There was an evening during that time when I expressed my guilt to my friend, Diane, who had brought her teenage daughter over to the house to babysit Tyler, so I could go to the library and study on a night that Dave was working second shift. After listening to me voice my concerns, she told me that what she thought Tyler would see was not a mother who was purposefully neglecting her child but rather a mother who was working hard to improve herself while trying to create more opportunities for her and her family. She said what she thought he would learn from watching me do this was how important hard work and determination are and how it would inspire him to follow suit.

Wow, this was a concept I hadn't thought of and welcomed with open arms. Considering that all this may benefit Tyler in his future rather than just being a void for him in the present was a much happier concept. With a new perspective, I breathed a sigh of relief, thanked my friend for sharing that advice with me, and headed for the library.

Being a lover of books and reading, not to mention the ambiance of a quiet space where other like-minded people gather to learn, the library has always been and remains one of my favorite places. I absolutely love to learn, and with their silence echoing with the curious minds of those seeking to soak up knowledge, the empty spaces are thrilling to me. There were many subjects I struggled with in college, and this quiet little sanctuary made it easier for me to study them.

Though I would sit and look longingly at the shelves of books I would like to be reading instead, I encouraged myself to concentrate on my homework with the mental promise that once a class term was over, I would come back and check out the book of my choice for a good long read. I tried to memorize the titles of books on the shelves that I wanted to read first. I could not have reading material available to me when classes were in session since I knew if I got started on a book during that time, I would get way too involved and be distracted from class and homework. So, to help myself get through to the end of each semester, I would tell myself that when class was over, I could read any book I wanted to. It was definitely a just reward in my mind.

I often reflect on that evening my friend inspired that different view on things for me, and think of the difference a short conversation spoken by a trusted friend, looking from the outside in, made in my life. It didn't stop me, though, from asking Tyler, when he was older, if he felt neglected as a toddler as I focused on myself. Did I make him feel second best in those days? He, of course, would tell me no. Nonetheless, I apologized to him, wanting so badly to ease my guilt and remind him he really was number one all along.

Judging by his stellar performance through school and college, my trusted friend was correct in her predictions. Tyler didn't have to be pushed to do his homework or sign up for classes. He was always on top of things. By the time I suggested he do something related to school, his answer would be, "Mom, I've already done that. In fact, some time ago."

So, I watched with envy as life carried on as usual for those others around me at work after I asked to be moved back into my past position. They, of course, didn't know what was taking place for me in my office at that moment. There was no reason for any interruption for them in their tasks. Their phone conversations continued without missing a beat. People on the other end of their phone lines' lives were the same as they had been moments before I surrendered, and office machines continued on with their duties for everyone in the department. I was devastated, again feeling like nothing other than a failure. I sat looking through the window of my office at everyone as life went on for them while mine had just stopped. All I wanted to do was sit and cry, but I wouldn't.

What I would do was finish out the day and go home to Dave. I honestly don't remember how I broke the news to him of what I'd done, but I know he was relieved. He had been concerned about me trying to handle this position in the first place and would have preferred that I not have taken it at all, though he knew how badly I wanted it. So, while I stepped back into my old duties, I kept working out of the little office I was using while supervising, since the department had no open cubicles for me to return to. It was a relief since when I worked in there alone; I imagined my inadequacies were less obvious to others around me.

So, life went on. I struggled to feel like I was contributing to those at work as well as at home. Tyler was going off to a four-year university around this time. Taking him to move and get settled into an apartment and a new life was, of course, emotional for us. This is what we do as parents, though, and I was careful not to cry when we prepared to leave him with his new roommates, some two hundred-plus miles from home. As we were leaving, I gave him a hug, turned away from him, and then back around, pulling him into yet another hug that was longer and tighter than the first one.

This was a new chapter for me as a mother, and it was as bittersweet as I'm sure it is for many parents. I think it may have been harder on Dave, no matter how he tried to play it off.

He and I returned home empty nesters, but proud of our son's new status in life. This took place in 2019, shortly before the pandemic. While I am thankful Tyler had a little time experiencing the dorm life and his travels by foot to classes on the beautiful campus he was attending, his time there was unfortunately cut short by the pandemic. Just as it was for the rest of the world, it was such a disappointing change of events for us. Especially so for Tyler, and I felt so bad for him. He was being robbed of an experience he had worked so hard for and would never be able to duplicate.

Chapter Twenty-One
Mystique

My treatments and work schedule continued as usual. What was unusual was that I started noticing I was dropping stuff and knocking things over. I couldn't gauge the sensation in my hands or realize when I didn't have a good grip on whatever I was trying to pick up or move. This led to many spills and messes as things slipped through my fingers and out of my hands. It was confusing and frustrating, to say the least. I discussed this with my oncologist during our monthly appointment.

As he listened to my concerns, he started nodding, a sympathetic look settling over his face as I spoke. He said I likely had peripheral neuropathy.

Wow, you mean this was real and not just a figment of my imagination? It even had a name. Never having heard of this, my doctor explained this condition is a result of your nerves getting damaged, and they then don't send information from your brain to your spinal cord properly. Some of its many symptoms include tingling and numbness in certain body parts or a loss of sensation in touch. He said in my case, it was probably brought on by a combination of my disease and the side effects of the medications I was on. He said there really wasn't anything I could do about it. This, of course, was disheartening; one more thing I have had to accept as part of my life with cancer.

I have since learned it is much less stressful (and a lot more fun) to laugh at myself when I drop, spill, and knock things over than it is to get angry. Not that there aren't times when I get so frustrated that I bend over, grit my teeth, and let out a vicious growl. Most times, though, I laugh, clean up my mess, and move on. One thing I know for sure is that there are far worse things in life.

I also experience nerve spasms in my lips and face that make them twitch. Thankfully, it doesn't happen often. There was also painful cramping in my hands that came about unexpectedly, and I was at a loss as to how to deal with them. My doctor suggested drinking tonic water. Thankfully, those don't happen often, either.

Another major event transpiring in my life at that time was that the financial institution I worked for, which is less than a ten-minute drive from my house, was going to be moving its headquarters to Santa Maria very soon. I would then be required to drive twenty-five miles each way, adding another hour to my workday. I can barely handle an eight-hour day now, and that's with knowing I can leave and go home at any time if I am having a hard day.

The chemo brain was still a huge issue. It was so difficult to concentrate on the issues customers were trying to explain to me during our phone conversations. Then when I go to respond, the sentences I have lined up in my mind to say are completely different from the ones that come out of my mouth. I had no idea where they were coming from. Not that anything I wanted to say mattered, as most of the time, I couldn't talk, anyway. My chest and lungs were always so full of phlegm I couldn't speak. I was constantly trying to clear my throat as I tried to talk, feeling sorry for the person on the other end of the line and those around me who had to listen to it. It was humiliating.

I couldn't retain the information or instructions from my bosses or coworkers, and I was constantly looking for notebooks (of which I had many) to write things down on. This, I know, is especially frustrating for my manager.

Along with my deepening lack of confidence comes more severe insomnia. I have been prescribed sleeping pills, as, along with the emotional issues I am dealing with, I am taking steroids once a week as part of my treatment regimen. It is near to impossible to get to sleep on the nights of the day I'm required to take them. These sleeping pills can be addictive and can also cause some pretty scary side effects—another thing to add to my list of concerns.

My distress at being able to perform at work (or anywhere, for that matter) was more than apparent, most of all, to Dave. He had been trying to convince me to retire for some time now, knowing it would be better for my mental and physical health. He told me it would be better all the way around for both of us. Dave retired on December 31st, 2019. It was mandatory in his line of work to retire at age fifty-seven. The fact that he already had twenty years in meant he could leave a little before turning that age. He was constantly trying to get me to come to my senses and see how much more damage I was doing to myself and the family by trying to hang on to something that obviously wasn't working for me.

"It's just bringing you down," he told me.

I knew he was right. I just couldn't and wouldn't admit it. He finally gave up trying, and we didn't talk about it for a while.

Come December, I once again felt cold symptoms coming on, just as I had in January of that same year. I gave it a week to see if those symptoms would subside, and when they didn't, I called my primary doctor's office again to see if I could be put on that day's call list. I soon got a call back and was given a time to come in. I had a sense of déjà vu, as my regular doctor was not available, the same as he had not been in January when I had come in with mild symptoms that turned into bronchitis, and I saw the same doctor that I saw on that day in January.

What was different with this appointment was that when I sat down to be assessed, I did not ask but instead demanded to be put on antibiotics immediately. I was not going to repeat the events that had taken place earlier in the year by sitting back to see how things developed. As much as I hate being put on medications, especially antibiotics, which kill off so many good bacteria in your body, I wanted to eliminate the bad ones before things got worse. The doctor did not hesitate to write me a prescription that day. I was well enough later that month to attend the employee's annual holiday party—my favorite event of the year. We had a blast.

One weekend in February 2020, we were part of a group camp-out, and Tyler, along with our niece, Hailey, had come from college to join us for a couple of nights. He and I sat next to each other in the group that had gathered around the campfire. I was describing the difficulties I was having trying to keep up with my duties at work and how depressing it was. Like Dave, he, too, felt I should retire. I told him I didn't want to, reminding him that I loved my job and loved to work.

"Mom," he said, "you just sat there and told me how depressing it is to you to go to work now and not be able to think straight. How hard it is for you that you used to be the go-to girl, who, in her thirty years with the company, had spent most of them in collections, where you felt like a semi-expert, but now you didn't feel like you knew anything about anything. You say you're afraid to answer people's questions out of fear that what you tell them might not be the correct answer."

I knew he was right, and I admitted that to him. If someone sat there and told me the same things I was telling him, I wouldn't understand why they wouldn't just rather remove themselves from that situation and focus on doing those things they enjoyed doing. I rarely thought about doing anything that didn't pertain to work, even on the weekends.

As I mentioned earlier, the financial institution I worked for is open half-days on Saturdays, and our department had to be available for customers during those hours. I often weaseled my way in during those days, whether I was scheduled or not. I remember one of those days, one of the employees in the department looked up at me with an exasperated look on her face and asked, "Don't you have any hobbies?"

I was too proud to tell her I had asked myself that question many times over the years. It just seemed that work, or any class I happened to be taking at any given time, kept coming back to be my hobbies. When I was in junior high and high school, my horses were my hobby. All I wanted to do during that time was to be with them and listen to my favorite music. Then, in my senior year of high school, my mother convinced me to allow her to sell the one horse I still had in exchange for her help to buy a cool car soon. I folded.

There have been a couple of times in my adult life that I have tried to relive those days and purchased a horse. Once, it was kind of an accident when I drove alone to a well-known horse ranch in our local area to see what it would be like to attend a live horse auction. Well, I found out all right! After getting caught up in my emotions when an Arabian filly was led into the sale ring, which reminded me way too much of our mare, Tammy, whom we'd owned not just once but twice before her passing, I lost control of my senses. My arm went up when the bidding got down to the amount that matched exactly with what I had managed to put aside in my bank account. I had thought someone outbid me, and with my broken heart in tow, I turned to leave the area so no one would see me cry.

Then I heard the auctioneer's voice say, "Sold for $700.00." The exact amount of my last bid.

I stood there in shock before turning and seeing the auctioneer looking at me. "Oh dear," I thought, "I think I might have just bought a horse." I really didn't mean to. Mind you, I was living at home with my parents, earning a meager income while working two waitress jobs and paying no rent. Not to mention I had just bought and brought home a Doberman Pinscher puppy my parents forbade me to have. In my defense, one of my friends had told me I could keep her at their house if my mom and dad absolutely wouldn't allow me to keep her at theirs. They did warm up to her after the shock wore off. Here I was, busy caring for a new puppy, and then I went and brought a horse into my life.

I was also trying to explain to the salesperson trying to collect my cash that I would have to come back with a check. "You can't do that," was the response of the cowboy in charge of sales.

"I have no other choice," I said. I certainly didn't come prepared to buy a horse, and I don't carry that kind of cash in my pocket. Especially when it was every dime I had. Besides that, I had no horse trailer or place to take her. I would have to secure a facility to board her and rent a horse trailer before picking her up. I really had myself in a pickle (no pun intended) and had to move fast.

Somehow, an arrangement was made to house this filly there on the ranch I'd bought her at for a couple of days while I worked fast to make arrangements for her boarding and rent a horse trailer. Thank goodness my cool car had a tow ball. Hoping that the cloth rag substituting for an oil cap on my car would hold up under pressure, I went out, again by myself, picked up my new horse, and took her out to the stables. What I didn't do was tell my parents what I had done. It was much too soon after bringing home the forbidden puppy, and I was concerned about their reaction.

So, for a couple of months, I kept quiet. Both my parents worked full time and didn't know what I did during my time off work. The perfect opportunity to tell Mom finally came one day, and I went for it. I was visiting her at her office, and one of her coworkers and we were having a conversation about all sorts of things. The mood was jovial, and there was the coworker I trusted Mom would not scold me too harshly in front of if I brought up the horse. So, I came clean. Her reaction was better than I could ever have hoped for.

She burst into an exasperated giggle and laid her head down across one arm on her desk while playfully pounding her other fist on its surface. She shook her head from side to side, playfully asking, "Why? Why?"

Her coworker, who was always one of my favorites, sat giggling, teasing us, and thoroughly enjoying the moment.

Whew!! I knew then that I was in the clear. Was I ever glad that was over!

Sadly, it turned out that the beautiful little filly at the center of all this was much more than I could handle in my life at the time. She was just two years old and not broke to ride. I lacked the time, the know-how, and the funds to train her. There was also my puppy, two jobs, and by this time, a boyfriend in the picture. Luckily, I was later able to sell her to a coworker, and I felt it was the right thing to do for everyone involved, especially my beautiful little horse. It was. The events that took place for me the day of that auction, and then later having to part with this horse, who, in my mind, had so much potential, did inspire me to write the following poem entitled "Mystique," which was the name I had given my little dream horse.

"Mystique"

What was the magic spell she portrayed in her eyes,
The day she pranced before me with her mystical stride?

The promise of a dream dancing on the end of a rope,
With the pride of a stallion, was a filly seeking hope.

In the brief moment, her leader stepped into this room,
Spread out before me, my irreversible heirloom.

Surrounding this pair was a misty, glowing light,
For only my eyes to learn her promised birthright.

An uncontrolled fantasy unlocked within my mind,
Now standing before me was a legacy that had been left behind.

Swimming in emotion, my eyes grasped her tight,

An unbreakable spell that encircled us at sight.

Still holding my ground while my head dropped to hide,
The memory of a legend, who ran wild at my side.

Mystique

Before I could move from this mystified stance,
I heard a voice call out to me as she continued to dance.

This voice called out so loudly that my senses did sway,
In a direction that is unanswered to me still today.

But how could I have held it hidden deep within,
When she so proudly painted pictures of my fantasies again?

Then, in a split second, while other chancers joined to call,
A hand I found to be mine waved up higher should it fall.

Faster than I heard one voice as my very own,
Came other countless callers, and my chances all seemed blown.

As I turned away, to run and uphold my spilling pride,
Of a princess who lived now, like my queen, no longer alive.

Dropping behind the crowd that shadowed this magic spell,
I suddenly heard my penny had hit this wishing well.

May I come to a stand as I look back to that time,
Since as I write these words today, she is no longer mine.

Through reckless tears and sleepless nights, I stumbled to the truth,
That I could not give to this princess what she deserved in her youth.

Handing to a stranger the rope that held my dreams,
I could only hope her pastures would be forever green.

Cut was the course that kept this beauty mine,
Only to know my fantasies never would unwind.

Mystique is the name this heiress still holds,
As she dances to her destiny as my queen of solid gold.

Sandra R. Pickles

December 15th, 1983

Chapter Twenty-Two
Light at the End of the Tunnel

Back at camp, I continued sitting before the campfire next to Tyler, who had just tried his best to make me believe in and accept what I already knew was true. Sitting across the fire from the two of us, one of my close friends, Michele, asked us what we were talking about. I told her we were discussing the idea of my retiring. She said I had her vote. She then said she really wanted me to come over and sit next to her. In my current state of mind, with the reality of the truth that I needed to quit working, I simply said I was exhausted and wanted to turn in. I needed to be alone. I believe it was then that I accepted my fate. Still, I just didn't know how to go into the office and say I needed to forfeit my job. It was so final. Where would I go from there?

To me, "retirement" was a dirty word that I didn't even want to know how to spell or pronounce. It was the last thing on my mind, and I remember when my mentor once asked me how often I checked my retirement account; I was embarrassed to admit I didn't know much about it. I wasn't even sure how to access the website on which the information was stored. He laughed, and I told him that, lucky for me, Dave paid attention to those sorts of things, and I was happy to let him. "Just let me go to work, bring home some bacon, and pay into my 401K plan" was how I felt about it all.

What would become of my life at fifty-nine if I wasn't going to work every day? One of my favorite things about working was the responsibility of being at a specific place at a particular time every day. Another one was dressing up and presenting myself in a professional manner. I enjoyed my routine of picking out an outfit and matching jewelry to go with it every day. My wardrobe was not complete without a dab of perfume on my wrists and behind each ear before leaving the house and driving to work, all the while looking forward to bouncing into the office with a smile on my face, humming and whistling to the tune of whatever song I had been listening to on the way there.

So, I continued to procrastinate and showed up to work every day, doing my best to contribute to the department in some way, shape, or form.

One of the ideas I had moved forward with before this time was testing out how my back and my health would hold up if I were to try horseback riding again. How would I hold up after the kyphoplasty?

I went online and did some research to find someone local who gave English-style riding lessons. Maybe you'd think riding English wasn't the best idea, as that is what I was doing when I was thrown from my niece's horse in 2012. Still, my passion for horses and riding always seemed to resurface, no matter the insults or injuries.

I remember an incident that took place when I was in junior high school when my best friend and I borrowed two horses that belonged to another member out at the Saddle Club, where my horses were boarded, so we could have my brother and his friend join us on a trail ride, using my two horses. I was on a thoroughbred gelding named Mr. Vista. The four of us rode for hours, going a long way from our boarding stable. It was a great time. That is until we headed home, and Mr. Vista, who, like my horse Thunder, had once been a racehorse, got spooked and broke into a wild run back to the stables. "No big deal," I thought. I had handled these types of situations many times before on my own horses. This was not my horse, though, and he did not react to my attempts to slow him down. When a horse is able to get the bit of their bridle clamped firmly in their teeth, it can resist the pressure you try to use in pulling them back. This is precisely what Mr. Vista did, and he continued at a dangerous speed. He was going so fast that my eyes watered from the pressure of the wind against them.

One of the primary fears when you're on a horse that's running blindly and refuses to stop is that it will run across a gopher hole or some such thing that might cause them to stumble or fall. God forbid a horse breaks his leg, as that type of consequence can often lead to them having to be put down. The second fear, of course, is what happens to you if the twelve hundred or so pound horse under you goes down. I have had my share of accidents with horses and was not anxious to have another.

When it became apparent that I couldn't stop him, I heard a voice in my head say, "Sandra, just hold on." The fact that I was riding bareback didn't make it any easier. Both my hands held a handful of Mr. Vista's mane, and I held on for dear life. We ran a long way, finally reaching the top of the hill to the boarding facility, where a dirt trail wrapped around the grounds. We had to go down and make a sharp left turn on that trail to reach the destination Mr. Vista was racing to get to, which was his corral, and he was still running at top speed.

All I remember saying as he rounded that corner, or rather tried to round that corner, was, "Horse, you're going to fall." That's exactly what he did, pinning the left side of my body under him before he regained his balance and bolted the remainder of the way to his corral. Not that I remember any of the last legs of his journey, as the impact knocked me unconscious. I probably wasn't out very long, but I remember the images in my mind of three horses running down a dirt trail toward me. I would later write a paper about this experience for one of my high school English classes, and this is how I described those images:

> *All I could see in my mind were three riders on horseback coming down a trail near the Saddle Club. The one in front was big and black and was racing down the trail, head held high, mane flowing, nostrils flaring, and muscles just bulging from his chest.*
>
> *He came running, leaping, dancing in front of my eyes in my mind.*

As I watched these horses racing through my mind, I was also hearing the familiar voice of my friend Brenda, along with another woman, who was also a fellow member of the Saddle Club. She had my head in her lap and spoke softly to me, telling me where I was, that I was okay, and that everything was going to be all right. She softly stroked my face and forehead, telling me that an ambulance was coming to pick me up and take me to the hospital.

All I wanted to do was lay there and sleep. I was so comfortable lying there on that soft cushion, a soothing voice in my ears, soft touches moving along my hairline, and the sun warming my body like a blanket. I didn't want to be bothered and was wishing everyone would just stop talking so I could continue sleeping. Too soon, an ambulance pulled up, and paramedics lifted me on a stretcher and put me in the back of their vehicle. I wasn't witness to anything happening around me as my eyes were full of the sand I had fallen onto. Thank God for the sandy conditions padded with grass that cushioned the impact when my body hit the ground with a horse on top of it.

I did come around on the way to the hospital but could still not open my eyes due to the sand that filled them. What I was able to do, was hear my mother's panicked voice as she and my father rushed into the hospital room, asking, "Is she okay?"

I felt so bad putting the fear of God into her. After all, it hadn't been that terribly long since she'd lost a daughter. I was fine once someone put eyedrops in my eyes and cleared them of the sand they were caked in.

I missed a week of school, as my left eye was black and blue and swollen shut. My left knee was so bruised it was psychedelic in color. When I did return to school, fellow students passing me on campus took a double take when they saw my face. Seeing their shocked expression, I would simply say, "A horse ran away with me and fell on me."

Most didn't comment, just hurried by with their books in tow and a horrified look on their face. Nothing, though, was bruised more than my pride, and I knew we needed to make amends with each other sooner rather than later.

A couple of weeks after this incident occurred, I spotted Mr. Vista's owner out at the stables. I walked over and asked if I could ride his horse in the arena. He looked at me with an expression on his face that asked, "Are you crazy, lady?". Nonetheless, he understood my need to get back on and ride his horse, so he threw up his hands and said, "Okay." Things would not happen that way today. Not with the liability concerns that come about when someone else gets hurt by your animal. I can't quite recall if I saddled him up that day or not, though I think I did.

Nonetheless, with my stubborn pride mounted firmly on Mr. Vista's back, we strode off to the arena. This was a large space surrounded by a fence, which would prevent another out-of-control cross-country race. Mr. Vista performed like a perfect gentleman during that ride, and we reached a subtle understanding with one another there in the arena that day.

I remember later overhearing one of the gals at the Saddle Club comment to another young member there about my determination to come right back out and get back on that horse after what had happened. I was kind of surprised that she was surprised. After all, we were riders, and in my mind, and I thought in the back of the mind of all other riders, it was simply a given. When you fall off, you get back on. No way was I letting my relationship with this horse, or any horse for that matter, end with a fall. I wanted to experience riding as many different horses as life would allow during my time on earth.

Anyway, my online search for a riding instructor led me to the home and business of a horsewoman who gave riding lessons and lived in the valley twenty-five miles or so from our house.

I sent an email to the address provided on the website and soon heard back from one of her associates. We set up a date and time for me to come out and meet with this person and see her riding facility. I couldn't wait. I shared this exciting news with my sister-in-law, Angela. She and her daughter, Cora, have horses, and she had included me in riding with her before my niece went to college and sold her mare. Angela asked if she could join me in seeing this facility and meeting the instructor.

I was thrilled to say, "Yes," thankful for not only the company there but also for the opinion of another horse lover. As July 1st is my brother's birthday, I will never forget it was July 1st, 2019, when we went out, both looking forward to our little adventure.

Meeting the instructor was a pleasure, and the three of us spent quite some time talking while she walked us around the training facility, answering questions and introducing us to all the horses living there. She owned some, and some belonged to persons she boarded to. She also had horses she had rescued and rehabilitated. This was the case with the paint mare she thought would be a good match for me in my lessons once she knew of my experience and what I was trying to accomplish now.

I let her know of the recent injury and surgery done to my back, the fact that I had not ridden in a long time, and was interested in testing not only my physical ability to get back into riding but my mental ability as well. Shay was this mare's name, and like me, she had overcome trauma. With the amount of time that had passed during the conversation between her, myself, and my sister-in-law and the fact that the sun was going down, the instructor asked if I was hoping to ride that day. I really was, and I asked if I could, even if it was only for a few minutes. I told her I was most anxious to see how my back would handle being up on a horse.

"Okay," she said, "let's saddle Shay up."

We did, and with the helmet required for all riders to wear in place on my head, I gathered up those reins, slipped my left foot in the iron stirrup of that English saddle, and felt butterflies in my stomach as I pushed off the ground with my right leg, swinging it up and over Shay's back, where I planted my behind. Angela snapped a picture of me up on Shay at that moment. When she later shared that image with Dave, he would study it a moment before saying, "Well, I haven't seen that smile in a while."

We made our way to the riding arena, where we spent a short time walking the ring, Shay and I getting to know each other a little bit.

I was on cloud nine, especially since I didn't feel any pain or pulling in my back that would cause me to think I should have any concerns about riding again. "I really am okay!" I thought. My riding plan with my new instructor was an hour lesson with Shay every Thursday after work. It was so exciting to have this to look forward to every week, especially with my continued struggles there. Those lessons became the light at the end of a seven-day tunnel.

Chapter Twenty-Three
Retirement

One Thursday, as I left work and headed home to prepare for my lesson, I saw my family working at our parents' house, preparing for the inevitable estate sale. While I knew this needed to be done, it was heartbreaking to see the garage door open and their personal items being pulled out and organized for sale.

To add to the heartbreak was a feeling of guilt as I stopped and told them I was scheduled for a lesson and couldn't help in the house that day. They all assured me I should go. The drive there that day didn't start out easy due to my emotional state, as I struggled to focus on the road. It soon turned out, though, to be precisely the antidote I needed to soothe my saddened soul.

As I drove past the horse ranches that lace both sides of the road I travel on to get to my destination (remember the ranch where I accidentally bought a horse), I felt my heart start to settle at the sight of the pastures covered with green grass and horses. The feeling got better as I took in the view of the sun shining down through the leaves and branches of the trees that lined the pastures. I listened to the rays of sunlight that spoke to me every passing mile of the drive that day, assuring me in soft whispers that things would get better and that one day, I would be okay. How I needed these simple but priceless pleasures at this moment.

On another one of those Thursdays, there was a situation with my brother that caused some intense anxiety for me before my drive to the valley. The feelings of frustration and helplessness drove with me there, parked in the same spot, causing me to approach my instructor and immediately lay my anxieties at her feet. She was well aware of the challenges I had been trying to deal with in life at the time, and she was generous with her ear and encouraging with her words.

Once I unloaded those emotions and calmed down a little, she asked, "So, what do you want to work on and have Shay teach you today?"

I looked at her and asked, "Can we just ride?" I did not want to be taught anything that day. I didn't want to focus on listening to anything but the rhythm of Shay's hooves as she moved under me.

My instructor looked at me with a smile. She completely understood the nature of what I was asking for and said, "Let's do it."

We saddled the horses, and rather than head for the riding arena, she took me to the fields beyond the ranch, showing me the lay of her land and telling me the stories behind it. We had a peaceful ride, and as dusk descended, we admired the sunset, riding until the light was no more. Best lesson ever!!

This schedule lasted until November 2019, when fall brought with it the time change, and my lessons ran into the dark of the day. During that time, though, I felt I learned a lot more about the style of riding English, which I love, and that I'd re-awakened my love for horses and everything surrounding them. It was, undoubtedly, one of the things my heart and I needed.

A couple of months after my riding lessons ended, I started talking with Angela about the void I felt and the idea that maybe I could lease a horse. She brought up the thought to the young lady who owns the ranch where she boards her horse, which is much closer to our home than the one I had been taking my lessons at.

This person said she did have a mare that she would consider leasing to me, and we met up at the ranch so that she and I could meet. I was cautiously excited, still very concerned about the risk of aggravating my back. Things seemed as if they would be good between her horse and me, and an agreement was made between the ranch owner and me for me to lease her. It got dark too early in the evening for me to make it out much after work, but still, I was so thankful for the time I had there on the weekends.

Unfortunately, this little palomino mare could sense my apprehension and, as many horses will (and most people do), took advantage of my weakness. She would act up, making me more cautious and concerned about getting hurt. After all my previous back injuries, my worst nightmare was to hurt it again and become unable to walk or, God forbid, be unable to dance. I decided not to push my luck and let the ranch owner know I was not comfortable working with her horse. She completely understood.

There was another gal who boarded at the facility there who had an older horse she thought might work out better for me. Her horse, Tiger, got less attention than she would have liked him to, as she had three horses she was trying to divide her time between. She was more than happy to have me try him as a lease option. With his sweet, gentle nature, Tiger and I were a much better match, and we both grew to enjoy our time together. Just being in his company while breathing in the smell of the ranch, horses, saddles, and leather made for the perfect antidote for me to continue trying to heal my heart. As fate would have it, from the area where this ranch is located, I could gaze across the miles toward the mountains that surrounded the air force base where my horses had been boarded back in the day and invite them into my memories as I rode now.

While often enjoying my alone time there, the occasional company of other riders when we met up in the arena, or went out on trail rides, was awesome too.

One day, while riding alongside my sister-in-law and the gal who owed the ranch, I listened to them compare the inconveniences brought on by not being able to indulge in their usual hair care routines since Covid had shut down beauty salons. One of them brought up her need for a good haircut, and the other brought up her need to get her hair colored. I simply said I was just happy to have hair. The conversation came to a quiet end there.

So now, back at camp, with the conversation that Tyler and I shared by the fire burning in the back of my mind, I also contemplated the fact that I was now having to work at the company's headquarters in Santa Maria. While working in the new lavish building was fun and exciting, it did make life more difficult for me. Most of those who worked in my department lived in Lompoc, and about five of us arranged a carpool. There were two different shifts we rotated on, one being 8:00 to 5:00 and the other being 8:30 to 5:30. This, of course, meant that everyone in the carpool had to be to work by or before 8:00, and stay past 5:30, whether you were scheduled for that shift or not. Add in an hour's drive time between there and back, and you're looking at a ten-plus hour day.

In my life BC, this would not have been a big deal. In my life with cancer, however, this was not an option. My body and brain could not deal with the longer days, and when it was my week to drive, there were times I felt like I was driving under the influence. It scared me, and it wasn't fair to me, those riding in my vehicle, or other people on the highway. I was also still losing a full day of work every week to go to treatment. I finally had to accept the fact that I was fighting a battle that was not only adding more damage to my health, both physically and mentally, but I was also a drain on everyone and everything else. What was the point of putting everyone through this?

Because in the same way, I had kept my problems and insecurities at bay in the past by obsessing over college courses and my career, I now tried to subdue my panic over what seemed to be a continuous decline of my health by keeping my mind busy with work.

Here was the same person who didn't want to know how to pronounce the word "retirement" and didn't like the taste of the word in her mouth when she said it, resigning to the fact that it was necessary.

The day I picked in late February 2020 to go in and let my manager know it was my intent to take early retirement still plays out in my mind like a dream. The hardest thing in saying this was knowing that with those words came a permanent end to my thirty-one-year career with the company, as well as no more significance to the bachelor's degree I have. Nor could I see anything that promised to be waiting for me at the end of the line after my two-week notice ended. Still, there was a peace deep inside me that said, "This will be the beginning of a new life for you and your family, and you and everyone you love will be better off now that you are heading there."

Once I had signed off on everything with human resources, I took the opportunity at our next department meeting to share the news with my coworkers. They had a nice lunch brought in for everyone on my last day of work, which happened to fall on Friday, March 13th, 2020. This was the weekend that then-president Donald Trump started shutting down the country due to Covid-19.

Some of my family members had planned to meet me at a particular restaurant to join in on a little retirement celebration for me, and the location had to be changed several times when we learned that one restaurant after another was closing its doors due to the shutdown. We were finally able to find a spot and enjoy a little celebration. It was a good evening. There were cute cards given to me with words of congratulations. One that reads in my mind often is one my niece, Hailey, gave me in which she wrote in big, bold letters, "You inspire me every day!"

The devastation that has followed the spread of this virus, as we all know, has been and continues to be beyond belief. While I missed working in those early days, I cannot help but feel that I couldn't have gotten out of there at a better time. With so many people losing their jobs and unable to pay their bills, my job collecting would have been even more stressful for me and my health. You would have thought I planned the timing of all this. I swear I didn't. I had followed the standard two-week time frame of giving my notice to leave, which in this case was the end of February, making my last day almost the middle of March. Thank God for small miracles.

There was a long period after I stopped working that I was somewhat depressed as to my new status in life and very angry, not only because of the fact that cancer had taken life as I'd known it away from me without my consent but also because it now had so much control over how I felt, how my family felt, and how we lived.

Who invited this damn disease here in the first place?? I kept going back to placing the blame on the devil, and I continued to curse him and all those others in my life who had ever had a negative impact on me. I knew this wasn't healthy, but it didn't seem I could help myself. I had a lot to be bitter about besides cancer, which didn't help matters either.

It wasn't just bitterness, mind you. It was fear. Just how long did I have to enjoy the retirement I didn't want to take before cancer caught up with me and put an end to that, too?

Shortly after Barbara had passed, I received a copy of her and her late husband Roger's death certificates. I tried not to focus too hard on the reality of what those documents said in their silence, and I guess I should have been more prepared to see what I saw when I reviewed them, but I wasn't. Like my mother, Roger had had several health issues besides multiple myeloma contributing to his passing. Still, there were just two words listed on that certificate as the cause of death, and those two words were "multiple myeloma."

As I sat there, trying not to let the words I read cause my soul to wilt, my memory wandered back to a conversation Barbara and I had had one day after my diagnosis while visiting her at her home. We were talking about Roger and my situation, and she said, "Sandra, Roger didn't die from multiple myeloma; he died from other issues concerning his distressed heart and internal bleeding."

There were other things going on with him health-wise, and I knew this. Still, looking me straight in the eye now was a death certificate showing the two words that identified the same disease I have as the cause of his demise. As disheartening as this was, again, by this time, I had become very good at not allowing myself to feel anything at all in these types of situations. It wasn't even something I think I shared with Dave.

When I retired, the coworkers who had been a part of the management program I had been involved in gave me a gift certificate for a body massage with a local masseuse. I really could have used it immediately, especially since my back and shoulders seemed so achy all the time. In the back of my mind, I asked myself over and over, "Are the aches and pains I'm feeling due to my cancer, or am I just sleeping in the wrong position and simply overthinking all of this?"

Multiple myeloma, being bone cancer, of course, causes damage to its victims' bones and other internal organs, so I guess I did have good reason to be concerned. Still, I kept my thoughts to myself, not wanting to give Dave anything more to worry about.

With Covid running rampant, my immune system being overly compromised, and the fact that these types of businesses were first in line to get closed down due to the virus, it would be a good year and a half before I was able to take advantage of that certificate and get my massage. It was great, though, and I continue with massages to this day.

Chapter Twenty-Four
Dream Writer

Luckily, I was still leasing the horse when I quit work, and now I had all the time in the world to go out whenever I wanted and spend time with him. Since the steroids and blood thinners I was on caused me to bruise if I so much as rubbed up against something, I took to wrapping both my arms from elbow to wrist in those bandages one typically uses for a sprain. Just saddling Tiger up could leave numerous ugly red blotches up and down my arms.

I felt so fortunate to have an outlet during this time of isolation our country was under. During some of those quiet times that I rode by myself, in my mind, I would write out the story I dreamed of writing one day, detailing my experiences of living with cancer and with life in general. I also thought of lines of words I would work into the verses of poems I'd like to put on paper that might somehow ease my pain.

This was a lifesaver for me for about a year, and I appreciated my time with Tiger. I so enjoyed my sister-in-law, who rode with me on trail rides around the property surrounding the ranch and used her truck and horse trailer to drive us to other locations to ride. We had a lot of great times. I did, however, have some other goals I wanted to pursue, so I ended the verbal lease agreement I had made with Tiger's owner, thanking her for her generosity in sharing him with me.

Writing became more and more important to me, and I began utilizing the poetry website I had joined more often, submitting more and more of my poems on it. Ideas for the book I wanted to write about my cancer journey expanded, and I became more serious about working on it. The turbulent emotions that continued to emerge on the roller coaster ride that seemed to never stop in my life gave me much inspiration for several poems I wrote during this time.

Those numerous events taking place in our world are so distressing to me. It seems unbearable to watch the news sometimes and witness some of the events taking place. In an effort to ease some of the pain I felt with regard to what I saw going on, I wrote this poem.

"Never"

Never in my life did I think I'd live to see,
the events that are unfolding here in the land of the free.

I watch in heartbreak as humanity dwindles right before my eyes,
The way that people treat each other makes me want to hang my head and cry.

Why do we feel so much need to tear each other apart?
How could there be so much hatred buried so deep within our hearts?

We write our lives out in detail and display it upon a global stage,
For the rest of the world to read through, and then rip apart each page.

A virus takes lives by the millions and destroys our mental health,
It has stripped the livelihood of the working poor while the rich expand their wealth.

The whole world watched in horror as a young man died beneath the knee,
Of an officer sworn to protect him, though he lay pleading, "Mama, I can't breathe."

So began a movement which in no way should ever stop,
Until everyone is given the same opportunities for which this country fought.

But it never will be possible for the people of this country to unite,
When all we have to depend on is a government that does little more than fight.

Like children in a sandbox, they throw dirt in one another's eyes,
To blind each other from the truth as they spin their web of lies.

Using words sharper than weapons, they spit in each other's faces,
Our country has been stripped of its integrity, respect, and social graces.

The human race has taken to the streets, burning people and property,
They stormed our nation's capitol and made America a laughing mockery.

Law enforcement lives are ended by the very folks they're trying to protect,
Other officers take their own in shame because they can't suppress the rest.

Our borders are wide open, and evil intentions follow among,
Strangers that exploit little children and peddle drugs to kill our young.

The same land where I once stood proud and sang "My Country Tis of Thee,"
Has turned into a place I no longer recognize and one I no longer care to see.

The American way has been stomped upon, its symbol burned and shredded like a rag,
It will take nothing less than an iron thread to sew back together our American flag.

Sandra R. Pickles

July 1, 2021

Another thing I did during this time was reaching out to the voice instructor I had been working with before when I was on disability. I asked for her forgiveness for abruptly stopping all contact with her in the past and asked if she had room for another student. She immediately welcomed me back with open arms. I was so grateful.

Along with getting on a weekly schedule with her, I revisited my dreams of one-day writing, singing, and recording a song of my own. I shared this dream with her, and she encouraged me to work toward that goal. She gave up some of her own time to help me. She introduced me to the owner of a local music store, who assists in music lessons and such, and accompanied me to a meeting with him to work on putting music to the lyrics of one of my poems. It is a project on hold, though I look forward to getting back to it once my health allows it.

This daydream of creating my own song is one of the most vibrant of the many fantasies I have had, and its pursuit is one of the most exciting. I have thought about this since my early twenties. When I took voice lessons and wrote poetry back then, I would, in my braver moments (usually those after a couple of cocktails), tell those around me to remember my name, as I was going to be a singer/songwriter one day. They, of course, didn't take me any more seriously than I did. Dreams do not pay the bills, and I didn't have the confidence it would have taken to pursue that endeavor, anyway. So, I simply wrote a poem about my daydream and called it "Dream Writer."

"Dream Writer"

Who are you to set the standards for what they call a dreaming fool?
So what if my workshop is some paper and a pencil my only tool?
You tell me all I ever do is sit and waste away the light of day,
You have no right to condemn me just 'cause you don't understand my ways.

Well, reality is everyone's option, so the choice is always yours,
But don't you ever wonder if your dreams can offer more.
It's my imagination that keeps my spirits up whenever I am down,
It's the friend I always turn to when there's no one else around.

It's the voice that sets my pencil writing with a flow of words,
That begins a creation of the verses no one else has ever heard.
Since my heart is all that guides the feelings I set into these lines,
It's the only piece of work I have to offer you that's mine.

And when I can hear a melody between the words I read,
I know then that I have reached the point of pleasure my heart needs.
I guess I'm just another writer living within a dream,
Of hearing my thoughts flow through the songs that people sing.

Sandra R. Pickles

September 7th, 1985

I was also afraid of how I would feel if I pursued that goal, the most important one to me, and failed. Then what? I would have lost out on one of my life's biggest "what-ifs" and would have been crushed. That would only prove the truth. That I just wasn't capable, and my dream could never be. I did have a few other what-ifs, but this one was my favorite, and I figured the only way I could hold on to it was if I never attempted it and, therefore, never failed at it.

My take on failure nowadays is different. Every failure brings new opportunities, along with the desire that there will be many more tomorrows to come to pursue them. I tried to capture that feeling in this poem.

"What If"

What if life were perfect in each and every way,
And we had nothing more to reach for beyond those things we have today?
What, then, could we yearn for if we had no need to want for more?
If everything in life were perfect, I believe then that it too would be bored.

Without another wish to wish, another goal in which to seek,
There would be no more questions asking for answers, so why then should we speak?
For it's in today's imperfections where life's "what-if's" all lie waiting,
Giving tomorrow an opportunity to make their realities worth creating.

If our visions of the future were already crystal clear,
There would be no need for new days to dawn, and there would be silence in our ears.

It's that constant dream of "what just might be" that lies next to me at night,
And stirs in me the desire to reach for "what-ifs" far beyond the morning light.

I believe if life was perfect in each and every way,
Then the brightest future I could ever see would not exist beyond today.
So, I think the best way to keep life moving in the right direction,
Is to welcome and embrace all of life's little imperfections.

Sandra R. Pickles

January 25, 2021

I also had thoughts of putting my cancer experience down on paper and into a book for others to read. This would be in an effort to give hope to others struggling with a disease or other obstacles in their lives. There was and is, however, that self-doubt that always seems to be an issue. Then I started reflecting on my own struggles in life, my sacrifices, and those of my family as I clawed my way through college. I came to the conclusion that if I were to put even a fraction of the effort into my personal goals that I had set into my college and career goals, there was probably a pretty good chance I would succeed with at least one of them, or maybe even more.

So now, rather than my past habit of using my cell phone while I was out walking Smokey to call and leave a message on my voicemail at work, reminding myself to follow up on something there, I am using the voice memos on it to record a thought, or a verse to a poem that pops in my head, that may end up embedded in a poem or a song of mine, or, of course, in this book.

Thank God for all those self-help books I've read (and there have been A LOT of them), along with numerous stories I'd devoured of people not only climbing unsurmountable mountains but who took control of their journeys and forged ahead. I admired these unsung heroes for the courage they may not have believed they had before they were faced with adversity but managed to find it, anyway. I cheered with each and every one of them as I read of their victorious outcomes. I prayed for every one of those souls whose stories did not end well and those of the families that grieved their loss. So, when I considered all the challenges I faced in a relatively short period, I thought, "What if I could inspire others the way I had been inspired by so many of them?"

If I could give hope to just one person and calm their soul for even a moment, I'd have accomplished one of my goals.

After all, though my college associate's degree is in business management, my bachelor's degree is in sociology. After having Tyler, I had a deep-seated desire to improve the world I had brought him into and switched gears in my career goals. I wanted somehow to help those broken people whose suffering drove them to hurt themselves or others, commit a crime and end up in jail or on the streets. The subject I chose to write my senior thesis on was why abused women stay with their abuser.

I have always been especially sensitive (as everyone should be) to children who are abused or neglected. That feeling was much more intense since I'd become a mother myself. Second to that concern was women who were abused. It only stands to reason that those children living in a household where their mother is abused suffer emotionally, even if they are not the target.

When I started writing that paper, I believed women stayed in abusive relationships because they did not have the financial means necessary to support themselves or their children if they left. By the time I finished my thesis, though, I had a different point of view. During my research and getting a peek into the minds of these women, I came to the conclusion that it is more of an emotional dependency than a financial need. I'm sure it varies from one case to another, and in many situations, women stay with their abuser because leaving them may have fatal consequences. It, unfortunately, is too often true.

Chapter Twenty-Five
Changes

Shortly after starting to have thoughts about writing this book, Dave and I took a trip to his sister Michele's house to attend an annual crab feed in her area. Dave's brother, Kevin, and his wife, Jill, also made the trip there to join in on the event. The morning following our arrival, they, Michele, Dave, and I sat in the living room having coffee together. We were discussing life in general and the numerous issues I'd been going through when Kevin piped up with, "I think you should write a book."

I could hardly believe I just heard him say aloud what I had been thinking, but not speaking aloud to anyone. I had mentioned it to Dave a time or two, but had yet to take it or myself too seriously. Now, though, hearing those words come from Kevin made me feel like I could and should do this. Not that I got started right away, mind you. Still, on that morning, it became a "maybe." After that conversation, it seemed Dave started pushing me on the idea. I had to at least give it a try.

So, with a few goals to work toward in my daily routine, retired life became a happier place to be. Not that I still didn't procrastinate on things I wanted to get done. It's just that now I had some goals set that were meant for me personally and not for someone else's benefit, which felt good.

Sometime around the middle of 2021, I started thinking about the coworker I had reached out to after returning home from my transplant in 2018. She was the person who had the same cancer I do and had also had the same stem cell transplant I'd had. It had been quite some time since we spoke, and for some reason, the urge to touch base with her became overwhelming. I texted her, asking her how she was doing.

It turned out she'd recently started having issues with her cancer again and had been put back on medication. She had a fracture in her hip and was in a wheelchair. She, in fact, had an appointment with her doctor, I believe the following day, to go over some more test results. We started keeping in touch once again via text. She was on disability, under so much stress, and as I had been, she just wanted to return to work. I told her how well I could relate to her feeling that way, but how much more important it was that she put her health and family before her job. Easy for me to say now that I've been retired for over a year.

We compared our experiences with the medications we were on, some being one and the same, and discussed their side effects. My friend eventually informed me that the drugs she was taking were not working, and her doctor arranged for her to have a second stem cell transplant at the same facility where she had had her first one.

I was glad to hear that and hoped to hear all about another success story from her soon. However, as I figured she and her family would be overwhelmed with doctor appointments and travel arrangements in preparation for her upcoming treatment, I decided to hold off on texting her for a couple of weeks.

At the end of August, Dave and I celebrated our 25th wedding anniversary by taking a short trip to the destination where we'd gotten engaged. I had reached out to this friend via text a day or two before that trip; however, I did not get a reply. I didn't think much of it at first, but became concerned when my second text also went unanswered. Hoping it was simply an overload of commitments on her part, I tried not to worry.

On our drive home from that trip, I texted a third time, asking, "Is everything okay?"

No answer.

"Maybe she is in the hospital," I thought. I decided to ask another employee at the financial institution where she was still employed, whom I happened to be on the phone with a few days after, if she had heard anything about this person's condition. In a foreboding tone, before I finished my question, her response was, "Oh, Sandra, oh, Sandra."

The writing on the wall was written in the tone of her voice, and my heart dropped.

"She didn't make it," she said. This employee told me that an all-staff email had gone out just days earlier, informing them of her unfortunate passing.

I was shocked and heartbroken to hear this news. What went wrong?? Unfortunately, I never found out because I did not know her family members or anyone else who I could reach out to for more information. Many of the employees that had worked with her while I was there were gone by this time, and I didn't know where to start looking for information. I prayed for her and her family, doing my best not to allow thoughts of my own disease and demise to come into play.

Around this time, it came to be that the hours-long immuno-therapy treatments I was having could now be given in the form of a shot in the stomach, which took just a few minutes to administer. This was definitely a change, and truth be told, I was a little disappointed. After all, these treatment days once a month were my time to get out of the house, spend time with the friendly nurses, read my books and magazines, and enjoy my carefully packed lunches. I mentioned this feeling to one of the nurses, who told me she also heard the same sentiment from some of their other patients. In fact, one of them actually opted out of the shot. He preferred to come in for the day, mainly since he lived alone and treatment day was a social event for him. I could completely relate. It was, of course, much more convenient for us for me to get a quick shot, be done with it, and drive home.

It was, however, a convenience that was short-lived. My cancer markers continued to climb, and my doctor took me off the oral chemo drug I had been taking and put me on a more potent pill. It did bring those markers down, but it also left me so drained and listless that I asked if we could try something else. We tried relying on just the shots, but around November, my blood work showed the cancer was progressing and that a complete change in my treatment may soon be necessary.

It didn't really surprise me. I had been on this regimen for two and a half years, and it was inevitable that it would cease to be effective one day. People had often asked me how long I would have to be on this treatment, and my only answer was, "I guess until it doesn't work anymore, and they have to try something else."

I felt fortunate to know there were other options available to treat my disease aside from this one, so when this news came our way that day, I didn't think much of it. While the doctor tried to explain the drugs he may recommend soon, Dave asked what would come next if those failed to make a difference.

At this point, the doctor explained another type of cell therapy showing positive results in patients with multiple myeloma called Car-T therapy. He went on to try to explain the process a bit. While it was good to know there would be something to fall back on, being one to try to be positive, I said, "Let's not worry about trying to understand that now. Hopefully, whatever treatment we try next works." The last thing I wanted to think about was having to go through another miserable experience like the one we had already gone through with the prior transplant that had given so little relief.

On top of all this, my doctor also let us know that he had plans to retire at the end of this same year, and while he would still be somewhat involved in the center, he would no longer be seeing me for my appointments. This was sad news as he was as much a friend to Dave and me as he was my doctor. He had seen us through those days during my initial diagnosis, which had been the most trying and traumatic. Still, I was happy to have had the opportunity to be his patient for this long, and we congratulated him on his semi-retirement.

So, while we knew changes were coming, we had no idea what those changes would look like. Assuming treatment would just be a different drug, maybe even again in the form of a shot, there are few words to describe the impact of the news we were handed at my appointment the following month, just a few days before Christmas.

I did my routine lab work, and Dave and I showed up for my appointment with my new doctor. My new treatment would go from immunotherapy, drugs that stimulate your immune system to fight cancer, to chemo infusions, which by my definition, are poison to the body and brain. I had had enough of how these drugs made me feel and had just recently started feeling like I was emerging from my brain fog from the stem cell transplant. I wasn't anxious to do it all over again, especially for an unknown amount of time.

An even more significant blow came when the doctor told me what my new schedule would look like. The medication would be administered in infusions, each taking a couple of hours and given on Mondays and Tuesdays, three weeks on and one week off.

"Are you f**cking kidding me?" I thought as the news casually handed to us, once again, made time momentarily stand still for me. "You cannot be serious. What kind of a schedule is that to have to live on? What about the traveling I had been hoping to enjoy in my retirement and getting out in the used motor home Dave and I had purchased last year?" I sat in shock as those visions dwindled before my eyes.

Wasn't it bad enough we had been in lockdown due to Covid since the day I retired, which had already limited travel opportunities for us? Dave and I were both devastated.

In September 2021, we took a trip in the motorhome to go see my sister and brother-in-law and my cousin in Oregon. My and my cousin Gaylene's birthdays are in September, one day apart, and we had made a plan to spend them together that year. We made a few stops along the way to see other family members and went to a few restaurants during those visits. While in Oregon, I started feeling a cold coming on, and though I thought it was getting better, in reality, it wasn't. The day Dave and I left to drive home, it hit hard.

"Here we go again," we thought. We stayed at an RV park that night, and my lungs were so congested and my cough so bad we were concerned we would need to find the nearest emergency room. That would have meant unhooking the motorhome and driving it to the hospital.

Thankfully, I did make it home, only to go to the doctor and be put on antibiotics again. Turns out I had Walking pneumonia and a touch of bronchitis. Here we thought we would be safe traveling in our own motorhome, with our own bathroom and bedroom to sleep in, and yet I still managed to get sick.

Back at my doctor's office, he said that he would have to get authorization from our insurance carrier for coverage of the new treatment, along with a test I would need to have done beforehand to be sure my heart was strong enough to handle the new drug. He let us know his office would reach out to us once they had everything they needed and that an appointment would be scheduled for us to see the office social worker, who would go over paperwork explaining the new drug and its possible side effects to us. I would have to sign consent forms to agree to them administering it. Also, on this day, when I was supposed to get my usual monthly shot, the doctor felt it best that we forego it. It wasn't doing the job, so what was the point?

While it would have been disappointing to me in the past to feel like we had made the trip there without my getting treatment, it really wasn't on this day. I went into my defense mechanism of mental and physical numbness to not only not allow this awful turn of events to take me down but also to be strong and positive for

Dave, who did not always look for the bright side of things the way I usually tried to. I will say, though, that this news hit me especially hard, and our drive home was a quiet and somber one as I sarcastically remarked, "Wow, Merry Christmas!!"

Chapter Twenty-Six
New Treatment

The idea of starting a new year with this new schedule was so depressing. Like before, I could not drive myself back and forth from treatments due to the concern of their side effects, so Dave would have to bring me back and forth and wait while I had my infusions. What was he supposed to do for several hours, twice a week, three weeks on and one week off while I was getting treatment? When the immunotherapy infusions had been an all-day thing, Dave would drop me off and return home until it was time to come get me.

That didn't make sense now, with the treatment time being shorter. It's a damn good thing I was retired. How could one work on a schedule such as this? It seemed like a full-time job just trying to stay alive.

We were soon scheduled for our appointment with the social worker, and Dave and I showed up at her office for our consultation.

She provided us with paperwork explaining how the drug worked and any possible side effects it may have. I was also given a pamphlet to calendar out each of my three-week cycles of treatments. One of the first things she casually mentioned once we were seated was that one of the most common side effects this drug has is its reputation for causing peripheral neuropathy. She casually went on to tell us that once the feelings in your limbs and fingers were lost, they wouldn't come back.

Wow, thanks for that! Again, I understand people who deal with these types of things get immune to the sound and effects of the words they deliver to patients who are vulnerable to the very things they're speaking of. Still, I wonder if they shouldn't be reminded once in a while that it's probably the first time the patient is hearing them, and take into consideration the effect the news is having on the person who has their truths to look forward to living with. Of course, I was already suffering from neuropathy and had learned to do my best to live with it and laugh it off. Now though, I was signing up for and consenting to a new treatment program that would deliver a drug straight into my veins that would almost definitely not only cause it to get worse but be the cause of something that would never get better.

Great!!

The blow to my psyche caused my eyes to sting. Dave and I sat through this short meeting, doing our best to understand what was coming our way and ask any questions we may not have thought to ask when my doctor delivered the original blow. I mentioned the two-plus hour time frame for each individual treatment to her, and she said it would only take that long for the first one or two treatments. After that, it should only take ten minutes or so.

What?? Good news for a change? We were elated. I felt better signing off on those consent forms. When we got home, I reached out to several people, letting them know of that little piece of good news.

Christmas that year was better for us than the previous one, when everyone had been locked down. We enjoyed gathering with the family on Christmas Eve and Christmas Day. Dave and I hosted a small group of family members at our house on Christmas Day for dinner, and the following day, my sister-in-law and I took her two boys out bowling. We all had a great time.

That is until a day or two later when I started coming down with cold symptoms. Back I went to my doctor's office, where I was again put on a ten-day cycle of antibiotics. After that, Dave attended a New Year's party, and a couple of days later got a call from the person who hosted it, informing him that several guests had called him with the news that they had tested positive for Covid. This caused us to cancel another family gathering we had been looking forward to attending at Dave's brother's home.

While this chain of events was so disappointing, especially after having missed out on so much during the pandemic already, and I was so angry about being sick again, I had to admit that the good times we had already been able to spend with family during Christmas that year, made it all well worth it.

On January 11th, I got a call from the nurse at the cancer center in the afternoon, letting me know our insurance carrier approved my new treatment.

"Thank God," I responded. Not that I was looking forward to pumping more poison into my body, mind you, it was more the thought that I had no treatment of any kind since November, and I suspected that my numbers were skyrocketing by now. I knew that, based on what seemed to be my constant habit of getting sick, my immune system had really tanked. The cancer center already had my first two infusions scheduled for the following week. Bless their hearts.

I had also been scheduled to have my heart tested. I made the most of the early morning trip to the cancer center by treating myself to breakfast and a movie after it was over. It was a charming date.

In mid-January 2022, Dave and I show up at the cancer center for my first treatment of the new medication. We thought about the fact that it would only be for the first two treatments that I would have to sit for two and a half hours for the infusion and then for another half hour to be sure I wouldn't have any significant side effects. We took comfort in what the social worker had told us about treatment time taking just ten minutes or so after that. With this in mind, I arrived happy, cheerfully telling one of the nurses how relieved I had been when I learned of this after thinking I would be in those chairs for several hours every go-round.

I'm not sure how to explain the emotional crash that took place for me in those moments that followed when the person I was speaking to set me straight on that other than to say it certainly wasn't the first one, nor would it be the last. She informed me that while the time it took for the actual dose of chemo to be administered would only take ten minutes, all the premeds, flushes, and fluids that were also required during the process would, in fact, take a total of two or more hours every time I had treatment.

Say what?? I was, here again, devastated. Here was the one piece of good news I thought would help us get through this recent change of events, being flushed right down the toilet. I had felt obligated to share the information I had been erroneously given with those who had tried to be supportive of me when I was taking the news of this new treatment program so hard in the first place. Now, I had to go back to them and correct myself again. Why had we been misinformed about something that can make such an impact on the life of a person with cancer? As I've said before, those dealing with the emotional roller coaster ride a disease such as this takes you and those around you on should not have to deal with the misinformation given by those who we trust are the experts. It truly shakes up our already interrupted lives.

There I sat, feeling that sense of positivity I came in with seeping from my soul. I didn't usually allow myself the luxury of self-pity, but this really hit me hard. As the head nurse strolled over to say hi, and ask me how I was doing, I went on to tell her about my new predicament. She listened to my concerns and complaints as she bustled about and said how sorry she was to hear that my cancer had taken such a turn for the worse. She also empathized with me about having to now be on chemo rather than immunotherapy.

Feeling that I had a sympathetic ear to share my misery, I continued complaining as self-pity started setting in. I felt a stinging sensation in my eyes as they filled with tears. "This is it," I thought. "This is where I will break the vow I had with myself and cry about having cancer and all those other things that had come along with it."

Had this nurse fed my craving for sympathy, that is precisely what I may have done at that moment, but she didn't. She went on in a matter-of-fact voice to say that many patients using this medication had good results, and she was happy to hear I had the opportunity to be one of them. She then moved on to assist other patients. Wow. So much for my pity party! I was almost a little offended. Why wasn't she feeling sorrier for me?

With no one else there to hear my woes, I turned my frustration inward, berating myself for being such a big baby, for thinking this nurse didn't have bigger problems to deal with and patients to care for who had worse problems than I did. How dare I look for sympathy when I should be counting my blessings that, at that very moment, I was being given medication that would fight my cancer. I also reminded myself how lucky I was to have insurance to pay for these treatments provided to me by professionally trained healthcare workers who oversaw my care while I was there and only had my best interest in mind. After all, not everyone is as lucky as I am to have access to such luxuries when they are sick.

Pain and suffering are on display everywhere in the cancer center, a constant reminder that no matter how bad you think you have it in life, someone else has it worse. That thought has helped me push through many hardships in my life; as I tell myself, if others can face obstacles far worse than what I am facing and get through them, then damn it, so can I.

I recall a moment I'd had one morning while showering, long before my diagnosis. I had been dwelling on a situation that had taken place where I felt I'd been taken advantage of by someone and made to feel small. I was upset with this individual, and as is typical, I drummed up visions of revenge against them, rehearsing the things I wished I would have said to them. I honestly can't remember what the situation was or who the person was who offended me, though I assume it had to do with something and someone at work. These visions played out vividly in my mind.

Then my anger turned inward to the person who was truly responsible for the indignation I felt. After all, it was, in fact, I who had allowed myself to be treated in a manner that led me to feel insulted and injured emotionally. As usual, rather than standing up for myself and expressing my opinion in a dignified manner, I just took it. As often is with many of us, I was my worst enemy. It's easier to blame someone else rather than take responsibility for what we ourselves are responsible for. I know that no one can make another person feel bad without their permission, yet I continued to allow it on a regular basis. I made a decision at that moment. "Nobody gets the better of me," a voice inside my head said. "F**cking nobody" was the words I used to complete that message as I stomped my foot, the hot water running over my head, heating my temper.

Years later, I would add three words to the end of that statement, and those three words were "not even me." In saying this, I again refer to how we are, so often, our own worst enemy. I was guilty as sin for doing this very thing more often than anyone ever should, and I needed to put an end to it.

A question asked by the author of one of the self-help books I read was, "Why do we berate and treat ourselves worse than we would treat someone else?" We wouldn't normally talk to a friend the way we talk down to ourselves when we're addressing our own inadequacies. Why do we feel that we are not as important as others?

It's the same kind of idea that has always struck me strange, in that a woman who smokes will put out the cigarette she has in her hand the moment she finds out she's pregnant. But not until then. Why?

Why is it that we don't see or think of ourselves as vital until we discover that we are carrying a life other than our own in our bodies? How does that person, who has yet to arrive, have so much more clout than us? Then when they do come, we identify ourselves, not by our own names, but as so and so's mother. Don't get me wrong; I felt so important knowing my body was the vessel carrying and building another little person. My mother was right; having a baby is usually one of the best experiences a woman can have. It's a glorious feeling when you know your body has created another body, and that body belongs to this little person that you are responsible for bearing, nurturing, and raising.

There have been many occasions since I made that vow in the shower that day that I've had to hold my tongue when I would rather have, and had every right to, lash back out at my opponent. However, it was in my best interest, and that of many others, simply to blow it off and let those indignities roll off my shoulders. After all, in my line of work, it was as much an art as it was an unwritten requirement of my job duties.

One of my favorite memories of a conversation between my mother and me regarding my job was when we discussed using foul language in the workplace. She innocently looked at me and asked, "Sandra, you don't cuss at work, do you?"

"Mother," I said, "I'm a collections officer; what do you think?"

Mom, bless her heart, always saw the world through rose-colored glasses. It was just her nature. While I was offended for her when she told me that some of her coworkers called her Pollyanna, at that particular moment, I understood their sentiment. Had I answered, "No, Mom, I never cuss at work," she would have wholeheartedly believed me.

So, on that treatment day, when I was being denied sympathy by the very person who I was sure would provide it to me in large doses, I reminded myself of my golden rule. "Nobody gets the better of me," I reiterated, "F**cking nobody. Not even me, and especially not cancer."

So, I dared myself to cry, sucked it up instead, and learned to live with the grueling schedule required to keep my disease in check.

Chapter Twenty-Seven
Bad Luck

Along with the modern medicine I was relying on, I had reached out to a couple of integrative doctors. I wound up adding two more forms of treatment to the regimen I was already on and a slew of expensive supplements. None of which were covered by my insurance. Still, I was willing to try most anything for a better chance at survival. I would drive fifty miles south, spend an hour in a hyperbaric chamber at one doctor's office, then go a short distance to another doctor's office, where I would get Vitamin C infusions. Those infusions took a couple of hours, so I was spending three days a week hooked up to an IV for hours on end. It's a good thing I love to read and write.

As you may or may not have noticed, I seem to have a lot of bad luck. The night before I went to my first session in the hyperbaric chamber, Dave and I input the address of the doctor's office into the GPS system, so I won't have any problems finding the place. I had gotten her address off the internet. The problem was this doctor had changed locations, and while she updated it on her personal website, Google still showed the old one. I had simply typed in hyperbaric chamber treatments when looking for this service, and I wasn't even sure of the doctor's name.

I pulled up precisely at my scheduled time of 9:00 a.m., to where I thought the office would be based on the neighboring addresses, drug my purse and backpack out of the car, and began walking. Don't ask me why I thought there would be a need to access the reading materials and laptop in my backpack while I was lying in a hyperbaric chamber, but I grabbed it just the same.

It was a few minutes of walking up and down this street before I realized there was no building number matching what I was looking for. I began to panic. I went into one of the medical buildings on this street to inquire if the staff there knew where this doctor's office was. The polite young lady at the window tried to help me by googling the address I gave her to see if she could locate it. Google, of course, gives us the same incorrect information I already had, along with a visual of the building that matched the address. The young lady swung her computer screen around so I could see it, pointed, and said, "It looks like this brown building right across the street."

I thanked her, rushed out, and ran across the road in a panic, backpack still hanging on my arm. It's heavy, and the strap is rubbing big red ugly splotches into my skin. Again, I'm prone to bruising due to weekly steroids and the daily low-dose aspirin I take. There are already faded spots on my arms that appear to be permanent. Every time I get more, I take to wearing long sleeves, as the marks look angry and ugly.

It turns out that the brown building I circled numerous times as it got later and later, and my panic rose higher and higher, was a building under construction, made brown by the cardboard paneling it was wrapped in. It probably had once been the building this doctor practiced out of.

Finally, I throw my purse and backpack onto a cement slab to call the doctor. As I look for her number, my phone rings, and her name appears on the caller ID. She reminds me of my appointment and tells me I am late.

Really??

I tell her I am here but need help locating her office. She gives me her current address, which is on the next street over. She says it is right across the parking lot from where I am standing. Okay, to the left of me or the right of me? She tries to explain. I'm still in the dark as I hang up and run off searching again. After one more failed attempt to get directions from some construction workers down the street, I cross over to my left, find more buildings housing medical offices, and start searching. By the time I see the one I am looking for, I am twenty minutes late, flustered, and concerned I am throwing off the doctor's entire schedule for the day.

She tries to calm me. This procedure is all about relaxing and healing, she explains. She had checked her website after our phone call, and she told me it does, in fact, show the correct address. I am apologizing, and she tried to make me feel better by taking some responsibility for the confusion, saying she usually calls patients the day before their appointments to confirm details. Still, for whatever reason, she didn't do so in this case.

I tell her it is par for the course for me, as this type of thing always happens to me. We're in a hurry to get this show on the road, and she asks if I have ever been in a hyperbaric chamber. I tell her no. She lets me know what to expect, and after I climb into the chamber and pop an AirPod into one ear, she hands me a plastic tube and explains how to put it in my nose and wrap it around my ears. She then gives me my cell phone and zips up the chamber. I spend the next hour listening to music, shaking my shoulders, tapping my toes together, and thumping my fingers on my chest to its beat.

When my hour was over, the doctor unzipped the chamber. She seems to giggle a bit as she tells me I did great. I had noticed her peek in on me through the top of the chamber covering earlier, and I assume she must have caught sight of me rocking out.

We wrapped things up there, and I was on my way to my next appointment. Thankfully, I knew where this office was, having been there several times. I spent the next couple of hours getting a Vitamin C infusion.

Tyler lives In Santa Barbara, and we had talked the day before about possibly meeting for lunch, so I was thrilled when that plan worked out.

We sat on an outside patio of a small sandwich shop, had a nice lunch, and visited. We made tentative plans to do the same thing the following Wednesday, as I had the same procedures scheduled then for the same time. It is a beautiful drive south to this city, and it has many more things to see and do than in the town that Dave and I live in. I looked so forward to these drives and my lunches with Tyler that I began referring to these days as my "well Wednesdays."

I also started following a diet I learned about from a family member that was supposed to help heal cancer. It was rigorous, and against Dave's wishes, I followed it to a tee. I felt sure that all these extra things I was spending a fortune on doing would work in my favor. It didn't. Not only did I drop a lot of weight I couldn't afford to lose, adding more fuel to the fight between Dave and me that I should not be following any protocol other than that of my oncologist, but three or four months into following this protocol, my cancer markers were going up instead of down.

"Are you kidding me?" I thought again as I sat in my doctor's office and heard him tell Dave and me this. Who was doing this to me, and why? I wish I could tell you how many times I truly believed someone had put a curse on me that was working and would continue to do so until I was dead and gone.

I had only been on this new chemo medication for five months. You remember, the one I was told was so effective on other patients. Yet, here again, the cancer was progressing. Yes, this was the same medication I complained about having to be on and dedicate so much time to in the first place. Guess that's what I get for complaining, huh?

What about the alternative treatments I spent more time on and a small fortune on having every Wednesday? It was now apparent that none of these efforts were working the way I had hoped they would.

The next plan of action the doctor brought up was the Car-T therapy we had discussed earlier. Dave and I had thought of this as a last resort in my case, so you can imagine how unsettling it was to have him bring this up. "Are you f**king kidding me?" my mind screamed out once again. It seemed ridiculous that this kind of thing kept happening to me.

My doctor went on to say that since it would take some time for this type of therapy to be arranged, I should look into deciding what facility I would want to have this done at and reach out to them now to make an appointment for a consultation. His suggestion made it even more evident how serious and time-sensitive my situation was, and I felt a wave of fury. Once again, the following statement screaming in my brain was, "F**king bring it."

The integrative treatments and the grueling efforts (hey, I'd sacrificed a lot of good meals while on that diet) I had been putting in to try to combat the very type of news we were being handed today made it that much more of a piss-off. It seemed it all backfired on me, and I cursed the devil once again. By this time, though, I'd learned that the harder life tried to shake me, the angrier I got and the deeper I dug my heels in. "Screw this shit," I thought. "This is war!"

"How," I wondered, "did the kind of anger that seemed to come about in me so easily and so often in my life now develop when I had been so sensitive and nonconfrontational in the past?" I had almost always backed down and turned the other cheek when confronted or cried when someone looked at me in a way that led me to believe they were angry or disappointed in me. That was just my nature.

When we were kids, my sister, Barbara, continuously took pleasure in trying to rouse my anger, picking on me, and trying to get me to fight back. I never would. When my pleas to her to stop went unheeded, I used tears as my savior. I would start crying just loud enough for one of my parents to hear me, and to avoid getting herself in trouble, she would stop, smother me in kisses and repeatedly say, "I'm sorry, I'm sorry, I love you, I love you." Each of those events ended with her solemn promise never to do it again. That is, at least, not until the next time.

It almost always worked, and even if it didn't, I forgave her every time. It wasn't just me she bullied. Barbara was a hellion who enjoyed causing trouble. She started more than her fair share of fights in the neighborhood, taking down both boys and girls in her path. Needless to say, not many of the neighborhood kids bothered me. They knew who my big sister was, and that I had a couple more of them at home and a big brother to boot.

So where did all this determination I found alongside my anger suddenly come from? In hindsight, which is always 20/20, I found it had been brewing a bit throughout my life; I just hadn't been aware of it. The more I thought about it, the more I realized I hadn't been a complete pushover in all those challenging situations in my life. I'd held my ground during those times when standing strong was the only way to acquire or accomplish the things that were most important to me in my life. Other times, it was when I was coming to someone else's defense. As I revisited some of those memories, I surprised myself with some of what I came up with.

As a kid, the biggest wish I had in life was to have my own horse. I am not sure how old I was when I started begging my parents to make that dream come true, but I know it was when I was very young. Really, all I needed to know was that my oldest sister Jeanette loved horses, and since I wanted to be exactly like her, I decided I loved them too and just had to have one someday. After my sister married and moved with her husband to another state, I was alone in begging my parents for a horse. The Air Force Base we lived on had a boarding stable for active duty and retired military personnel, and it was dirt cheap to board a horse there.

My dad would not hear of us having our own horse, but that did not stop me from crying and pleading with my mother to get him to change his mind. I would look at the daily newspaper and local Easy Ad pamphlet that advertised horses for sale, go into my parents' bedroom after school while they were at work, lay on their bed, and make phone calls to those people selling their horses. I would ask all kinds of questions about the horses they advertised. How much they were asking for them, why they were selling them, how old they were, and even their names. Geez, what a pest I was.

My dream of getting a horse finally came true when I was about twelve and in junior high school. The first horse we got we bought in partnership with another family, and my mother did this without telling my father. She told him while we were at the dinner table the night the spoken offer had been made with the seller, but no money had yet changed hands. I don't know how long I held my breath waiting for him to kill the deal. Dad didn't say a word, and in his silence, we became half-owners of a thoroughbred gelding named Thunder.

We hadn't had our new horse but maybe two weeks when he unexpectedly made a dash downhill into his corral when Barbara and I returned to the barn after a jaunt around the stables. We were riding double, using nothing but a halter, Barbara riding in front, me behind her. Thunder was evidently in more of a hurry to eat than we thought, and when we pulled him to a stop in front of the barn, he bolted down to the corral.

Taken totally by surprise, we tried to hang on during that short dash. Barbara probably would have stayed on, but I lost my balance and hit the ground. Before I did, though, I unknowingly grabbed her by the hair in my desperate attempt to hang on, pulling her off with me while taking out a handful of her hair. She sat in the dirt pouting, pulling out more loose strands of hair off her head while scolding me for what I'd done.

I tried to use my hands to get up. My right hand hung limp and felt tingly. I looked over at Barbara, held my arm out, and said, "It's broken."

She, of course, was more concerned with how she felt. When our parents came to pick us up, we explained what had happened.

Against my dad's wishes, I was taken to the base hospital for X-rays. He hadn't wanted to make the trip because he didn't believe my wrist was broken. As it turned out, it was, in fact, badly broken. I had put my hands out to brace myself before hitting the ground, and my wrist bone was completely cracked.

To this day, I will tell you that the worst pain I've ever experienced was when the doctors pulled on my hand the following day, when they set the bone to prepare my arm for casting. This was after giving me shots of anesthesia in my armpit.

Still, two weeks later, with my right arm in a cast, I was back out riding Thunder on the trails. I'm still trying to figure out how my parents allowed this. I had been given a pass to be excused from my physical education classes at school since I couldn't participate due to my injuries, yet here I was, out riding my horse. That class was one of the last ones of the day, and sometimes I would leave campus before school ended. Since Thunder was my pride and joy, I somehow found a way to the stables and rode him back to the school grounds so I could show him off in front of those students who were sitting on buses, waiting to be taken home. Today, I would be suspended for that.

Sharing a horse with another family did not go over well with me, as I was jealous of the time they and their friends spent with him. I, of course, wanted him all for myself and Barbara. Eventually, the other family lost interest, we bought out their share, and Thunder became our own.

We would later get another horse, a Quarter and Arabian mix mare named Tammy. This came about when my mother had learned through her work of a person whose daughter had to sell her horse, and Mom decided that since Barbara and I had to share one horse, a second one would be nice to have.

In the past, Tammy had been injured in an accident while being trailered somewhere. She was left with a long scar running down her face and a fear of getting into a trailer again. She would not load into a traditional trailer when the current owners tried to load her up to move her from their stable in town to our boarding stable on base, about a fifteen-mile drive. After many failed attempts to coax Tammy into this trailer, she grew more fearful and agitated, actually yanking out a board she was tied to off the family's porch. Finally, the gal selling her said, "That's it. I can't do this to her. She is going to have to stay with me."

"Oh no, there has to be another way," I said.

So, a friend from the base stables volunteered to trailer her horse to the seller's stable and ride the fifteen miles back to the base with either me or my sister Barbara and Tammy. If memory serves me right, it was Barbara who got to take that ride, as she was a couple of years older, and my mother was concerned about the distance and the fact that we would have to cross the highway at some point. I was so excited to get another horse, and as we drove from town to the base that day, I looked out across the trails, trying to spot the two riders heading to the Saddle Club. That ride took many hours. I was so appreciative of our friend's generosity in making that trek. Now Barbara and I both had a horse to ride. We had many adventurous times together, and our two horses adored each other.

Chapter Twenty-Eight
How Life Works Out

Another goal I never meant to set but eventually accomplished, nonetheless, was earning two college degrees. You may remember my love of writing poetry and dreaming about writing songs. English had been my favorite subject in high school, and since I really enjoyed reading and writing, I enrolled in an English class at our community college. If I was going to write, I needed to learn proper grammar. What the heck is a hanging participle? What is a compound verb? I'm still confused.

When I graduated from high school, I vowed I would never step foot in a classroom again. I despised it that much. During my senior year, I put an abundance of effort into those classes that were required for me to graduate. I wanted to pass and be done with it forever. Still, here I was. Now, though, I was there on my own terms and only because I wanted to be. Hopefully, I would do better in college than

I had in high school, where my grades had been dismal, to say the least, even when I honestly tried to do well.

When I signed up for this class, I was working for an aerospace company on base. A couple of girls I recognized from the base were also attending this class, though they worked for a different contractor. The three of us acknowledged one another, and one of them asked me what my major was. I shrugged my shoulders and said, "I don't have one."

"Then what are you doing here?" she asked.

I told her that I was just trying to learn to write properly. Then, with that question burning in my ears, I turned around, faced the front of the class, and thought, "Yeah, what AM I doing here?"

That question changed the trajectory of my life. (Who was that girl anyway?) I was never even sure of her name. What I am sure of is that trying to satisfy my mind with an answer to that question pushed me down the path that started my college career.

After finishing that English class, I went on to attend even more classes, signing up for those offered in the evenings since I worked full time during the day. I found I enjoyed being in a classroom environment and being part of a group of like-minded people who were trying to better themselves. It made me feel better about myself. I enjoyed listening to the voices and opinions of other students and felt important when others turned their attention to me to listen to mine. I hadn't had the confidence ever to speak up in school before, and now I was doing it on a regular basis. Another surprise was that my grades weren't half bad. What a change from when I was in high school.

My confidence grew, and I enjoyed a sense of accomplishment that sent me back into the lines those serious students were standing in to sign up for classes that would begin the following term. That line eventually led to my walking in a graduation ceremony at that community college, where I would collect an associate's degree in business management.

Many years later, I decided to sign up for classes at a four-year university. Never, ever will I forget the feeling of pride when I entered the office of that college, with the knowledge that I was someone who was eligible to be there. I was in disbelief that I had arrived or that I would have ever arrived at a place like this in my life. While I signed up for more classes in business, after having Tyler, I would later change my major to sociology and earn a bachelor's degree in it.

Speaking of Tyler, having children was another thing I had not thought I wanted to pursue in my lifetime. I had long been hesitant about the idea and had, in fact, come to the conclusion that I may not want kids. Not only because of the heartaches I had watched my mother go through with her children, but also because of the horror stories I'd heard about how painful childbirth is. One day, though, a thought occurred to me that made me feel a little ashamed of myself. "There are billions of people in this world," I thought, "and a woman had to give birth to every single one of them." If all of them could do it, then damn it, so could I.

I was late in finding my true love in life. As I said, I'm very good at procrastinating. Dave and I met when I was thirty-four, and we married a couple of weeks shy of my thirty-sixth birthday. I was thirty-eight when I gave birth to Tyler. I enjoyed a pregnancy with no complications with him and went home from the hospital the day after his birth. A couple of years later, we tried again.

Sadly, the ultrasound results of our second child did not show as promising of an outcome as did my first, and the doctors were concerned from the get-go. They expressed those concerns to Dave and me, and while we were devasted, we were not surprised when things did not work out and we lost the pregnancy. That loss took place in a hospital fifty miles from home, where we spent three days in a room where I lay in bed, Dave sitting by my side in a chair by day and doing his best to get comfortable enough to sleep in it at night. Neither of us got much rest during those days, and we were both as physically drained as we were mentally exhausted.

Adding to our emotional distress were the phone calls coming in from concerned family members asking what was happening and if we were okay. We had left town abruptly. We were able to get through to Dave's mother to make arrangements to leave Tyler in her care and let her know where we were headed, explaining that we were having complications with the pregnancy.

My mother found out later and was determined she and my father should be there with us. We told them under no circumstances did we want company during this time and to please not make the hour drive to the hospital. Unfortunately, Mom did not take heed and had Dad drive them to the hospital anyway.

We got a call from the receptionist at the front office, informing us that my parents were there to see us, and they needed permission from us to allow them up to our room. Dave told them no. My father got on the line to speak with me, using that calm and loving tone he knew always worked on me. The only thing I could tell him, though, was that we were hurting and did not want to share what we were going through with them or anyone else. I was trying so hard to not only be strong for Dave and me but also to be firm with my father since it is so hard to say "no" to a concerned parent's request. When he knew my mind was made up, he put my mother on the phone.

It was upon hearing the pleading tone in her voice when she said she just needed to see me that my headstrong heart gave way. I broke down in tears, telling her how sorry I was that this was happening, but that I didn't want to see anyone. In that same way, I had wanted to share my joy with her when I had my first ultrasound with Tyler, whose birth had, of course, been joyfully triumphant; I did not want to involve her in the misery of the loss currently taking place. Finally, after pleading with her to understand, they accepted our decision, hung up the phone, and headed home.

After that, nature took its course, and we mourned for the life that should have been our second child and Tyler's little brother or sister but wouldn't be, now or ever. We cried not just for our loss but for Tyler's, too, though he, of course, could not know of it at the time. I thanked God he was too young to understand any of this, or why I was so sad in the days that followed our return home from the hospital.

I cried, remembering the image of our baby moving during the ultrasound I'd had done. It had been a recommendation due to my age. I'd had an ultrasound done for the same reason when I was pregnant with Tyler. The difference between the two was that everything with my ultrasound of Tyler came back with glowing reviews from the moment it started.

My mother had joined me for that appointment to be a source of support since Dave was working. I, of course, had never had this type of procedure, and while I don't recall that I was concerned, the company on the hour drive there and back was lovely, and the thought of having a trusted hand to reach out and hold should I need one, was comforting.

I will never forget the moment Tyler's image came up on the ultrasound screen as I lay on that hospital bed, and I could hear his heartbeat. I lay there in awe for a moment before asking the nurse if she would be so kind as to ask my mother, who was waiting in the waiting room, to join me at my bedside. She did so, and Mom came tiptoeing in.

I looked up at her as she crossed the floor and asked, "Would you like to see your grandchild?" We had opted not to find out the sex of our baby, so grandchild was the only description I could give her at the time.

She smiled in anticipation, sat down, and looked at the image of that very active baby swimming inside me, giving a little gasp as tears flooded her eyes. She looked at the expression on my face, which had to have shown how humbled and proud I was to see the evidence with my own eyes of the life growing inside of me.

When Mom was able to compose herself, she told me that when the nurse came out and told her I wanted her to join me, she thought maybe it was because I was scared. I told her no; I just knew how special it would be to the both of us to share this momentary miracle of my baby's first sighting with her, and I was so excited that I could make that happen. I was beyond happy.

Now, though, Dave and I held each other, trying to absorb the magnitude of the loss we were taking. The nurses asked us if we wanted to hold our baby, and at first, Dave and I had reservations about it. The kind nursing staff encouraged us to do so, explaining if we did not, we would probably regret it, being left to always wonder what our baby had looked like. They told us that some couples in this type of situation who chose not to see their babies later shared that they had dreams of what their disfigurements might have looked like. Wondering if they resembled monsters, images that might always haunt their sleep and subconscious. They reminded us that once we left the hospital, we would never have the opportunity to change our minds.

I can still hear the voice of the kind nurse who sat rocking in the chair beside my bed, holding that little body wrapped in a small blanket. She cradled it in her arms as she rocked, speaking softly to it and us, gently trying to soothe our souls in hopes that we would summon up the courage not just to look at, but also to take our baby in our arms and hold it. She encouraged us to take our time in making this very emotional decision, and she continued rocking. Once we decided we did want and need to see the baby who would not be coming home with us, she encouraged us to take whatever time we all needed to say hello and goodbye to each other for the first and last time.

This wonderful nurse lovingly laid him in my arms. We had tentatively picked the name Seth for our second child if we were to be blessed with another boy, and it was now evident that we would have been. I cradled the lifeless beginning of his body and soul in my lap in the dim hospital room, Dave sobbing beside me while he held the both of us. It was the first time I had ever seen him cry.

The only part of Seth that would come home with us, aside from those memories in our hearts, was an imprint of his webbed hand and footprints on paper. They did prepare a little memory certificate for us with his name on it. Those, along with a little cap and a little sliver of a blanket, got tucked inside a blue, circular wooden case that the hospital staff had been kind enough to put together and give to us. This case rests in the nightstand next to our bedside.

Seeing the emotional state of mind we had been in while holding Seth in that dim room, our nurse asked if we would like to have a visit from the priest that volunteered at the hospital. While Dave and

I are not active church members, we were raised Catholic, and we said, "Yes," hoping it would provide us some comfort. So, while this wonderful priest blessed Seth and the two of us, I expressed not just the grief I felt for our little family, but also the guilt I felt for the rest of our families. I shared with him how terrible I felt for not allowing my parents up to the room to see us when they came, especially after they drove an hour to get there.

He held my hand and asked, "But what about you and how you felt when you had to not only make that difficult choice but when you had to tell them of your decision?" He said that the choice was rightfully mine to make and that they should have honored my decision when I asked them not to come in the first place. He held my hand, trying to console me, telling me I had to think of myself, not just of them, and to think of myself before them.

This was the first time in my life that I felt like I had been given permission to not only think of myself at all, but also think of myself *first* while making those decisions that served me best. "Wow," I thought, "you mean I am an important enough person that I can tell someone else 'no' when I want to? Even when they keep asking me the same questions over and over, I don't feel comfortable with or want to answer?"

Why yes! Why, yes, I am, was the truth he convinced me of on that day.

While I embraced this new and fascinating concept and held onto that strength when I asked friends, family, and coworkers to respect my privacy and not bring up or ask questions about this situation when I returned home and went back to work, I would eventually fall into old patterns of worrying more about the next person and putting their wants and needs before those of my own. During that time, though, I did stand firm in saying "no" when people asked me to talk about what happened, reminding them of my request for privacy.

Time has mercifully eased the passing, and some of the memories of those days that served as the reality of that inevitable loss that took place for us then. Even though we knew we would be leaving empty-handed, we were anxious to get back home to not only our lives but to that of our son's.

I remember Dave getting me home and then leaving to go to his parents' house to pick Tyler up, as he had been staying with them for the three days we'd spent in the hospital. Tyler was just a couple of years old when all this took place, and I remember resting on the couch when he and Dave got home, and the front door flew open. Tyler ran toward me, excitingly shouting, "Mommy, Mommy…!"

I never asked him, but I'm sure Dave had done a little coaching with him before opening the door to let him see me for the first time in days. God, how good it felt to sweep our sweet little boy up in my arms and hold him up tight with me on the couch. The same couch the two of us had slept together on for months after his birth when he was so colicky, and the two of us were home alone while Dave worked out of town. I don't know how long I held him hostage there with me before letting him down.

Still, we kept trying to give Tyler a brother or a sister. Once we felt we had our emotions in check from the last attempt, Dave and I made an appointment with a specialist to discuss what had happened and what, if anything, we could do to have another baby successfully. We did get answers to some of our questions, which provided us with a bit of hope.

We had decided before we got married that if we were going to have children, we would have at least two. We both grew up in large families and didn't want our child to grow up an only child. Going forward, I would, in fact, conceive two, if not three, more times. I did not share the fact that I was pregnant at those times with anyone other than Dave and my two sisters. By this time, though, I was in my early forties and seemed unable to carry the pregnancies through. With the last one, I had been far enough along that I had to go in for medical care after my doctor could not detect a heartbeat during a routine visit. We were crushed.

The morning of my appointment, I sat on the couch, dressed and ready to go, and Dave walked across the room, heading over to open the front door so we could leave. He looked at me sitting there and asked if I was ready. I could only look at him and nod as the tears that had gathered in my eyes spilled over. I had been sitting there dwelling on the reality of where we were going and what had to be done. As my pain and feelings of failure rolled down my face in the form of teardrops, it struck a chord in his heart. "That's it," he said. "I can't put you through this anymore."

So, the decision was made with those words at that moment that we would not try again for another child. We felt blessed to have who we have in the one child we love so dearly, and we are happy with that.

It is funny how life works out. When Tyler was maybe three or four, he said he would like a little brother or sister. When he was eight or nine, though, and we asked him the same question, it was a definite, "Oh, hell no." I guess by this time, he was enjoying the fruits of not having to share the little extra bonuses that come along with being an only child. Who knows, maybe it was also just a bit of "he didn't have to share us with anyone either."

Chapter Twenty-Nine
Tears for the Soul

Two decades later, in my early retirement, I joined an online poetry site to see if my interest in writing would reignite and if I could still put poetry together like I had in the past when I was so very, very emotional. Though I did not take the time to explore all the different things the site had on it, I did take notice of some of the contests being offered to members on the home page.

There were many subjects to write on with varying rules to follow. You could enter some with pre-written work, and some would only allow a newly written poem to be entered. The contest that caught my eye was one where the host wanted newly written poems about being an only child. Well, I was far from being an only child, but I was the mother of an only child. I am so thankful for and happy with our one that I decided I would write about that. So, while I did not win the contest, I was still pleased with the outcome of the poem I wrote.

The Luck of The Draw

"My Only One"

I thank God for the day He blessed me with a healthy son,
And it may be a blessing, too, that he is my only one.
For all the times I tried to give to him a sister or a brother,
It eventually became clear that there just was not meant to be another.

I couldn't help but feel a void for you, an only child,
Since I grew up embraced by siblings where love and laughter grew wild.
In your youth, son, you said to me you'd make a good big brother,
You couldn't know my heartbreak in trying to again become a mother.

It wasn't that my love didn't ignite the candle for another life,
It just wasn't in God's game plan; something simply wasn't right.
So, God chose for me you, you see, to be not just my only son,
He chose that you would be so special that He could only give me one.

Sandra Pickles

July 19, 2020

I thought, too, about the determination that came about while I was single and living in the condominium my parents helped me buy. I worked two jobs but struggled to make my mortgage payments as my income was still below the poverty level. I figured the only way my financial situation would improve was if I were to get better educated. My goal was to qualify for a job that paid well enough so that I would only have to work one job and still be able to meet my monthly bills.

So, I started taking classes again at the community college. In order to get through school quicker and earn a degree, it would have been nice to have taken eight-week courses. However, eight-week classes were offered either Monday and Wednesday nights or Tuesday and Thursday nights, and since I was scheduled to work Monday and

Tuesday nights, I had to opt for sixteen-week classes that were offered once a week on Wednesday or Thursday nights.

My college career went on longer and stronger after Dave and I got married and Tyler was born. I had my associate's degree by the time Dave and I met and was, in fact, enrolled in yet another class at the community college, working to fulfill those courses required for me to move on to a four-year university. Though I did slow up on my school schedule for a little while after we met, I was soon back at it, taking one course at a time.

I worked through classes while pregnant with Tyler and started them back up after a short break following his birth. During those college years, most of the time I took off from work was to do homework or study for tests. In trying to complete my senior thesis for my bachelor's degree, I spent three days locked in our home office in my housecoat, trying to finish that paper before the deadline. I hardly showed my face from behind that door. I lost three pounds and don't think I showered every day. I was so stressed out about school. I often spent my time on the weekends studying. That meant missing family events I really wanted to be a part of.

Before the computer class ended that I was attending, when I learned of my diagnosis, I had bowed out of plans to go to plays with my mother a couple of times. Talk about feeling guilty, especially since Dad had been the one to go with her in the past but was now, of course, gone. Luckily, Mom had lots of friends and was able to find substitutes. Mom did ease my guilt some of those times, when after I begged for her forgiveness while explaining I just wasn't going to make it through this class if I didn't spend the day working on homework, she would say, "Well, I admire your determination."

What made me feel even better was when I told Tyler one day that my mother often said that to me when I was trying to get through something challenging, and he immediately responded with, "Well, she's right."

There was one particular assignment in that computer class I was trying to get through that I just couldn't seem to conquer, and when the deadline to submit it came around, I simply said, "Screw it." It was a Friday night, and I was sick of being stressed out and left out of the things I wanted to be able to enjoy on the weekend.

During the hours the deadline for submitting that assignment came and went, Dave and I were sitting at a local restaurant with a group of friends having dinner and drinks. The deadline danced through my mind, along with my margarita. This particular restaurant does have the best ones. At that moment, I can honestly say I didn't care if I ever turned that assignment in (and I didn't). I was that mad. I was in a constant state of panic trying to get through this course, and Dave begged me to drop it. Again, I probably should have. It would have alleviated a lot of stress for both my family and me.

Still, I was six or seven weeks into this sixteen-week course and knew if I quit now, I would probably never sign up for it again. More haunting was that if I did, I would have to relive the weeks I had already endured. I showed up to class once a week and felt like the biggest moron ever, as the teacher tried to help me even after she and the other students ran out of patience with me.

One night, I asked a question (one whose answer I had probably already been told a million times), and the teacher really did lose her patience with me and came across in a condescending manner. I can't blame her, but still, I lost it. I didn't say a word, just got up, packed my things, and walked out of the classroom. I got to my car and wondered what to do. I didn't want to go home and admit to Dave and Tyler what had happened. I can't really remember what I did, but eventually, of course, I went home. I'm still trying to figure out if I ever told Dave about that incident.

The following week, I arrived early to class, as usual. There were just two students there when I stepped in, two young men in the middle of a conversation that abruptly stopped when they saw me. I suspected they were talking about me, but I really didn't care. After a moment of uncomfortable silence, as neither one of them had yet to take their eyes off me, one of them said, "I'm glad you came back." I was pleasantly surprised to hear him say this.

"Thanks," I said, "I appreciate that." He, like me, was a bit older than those students who made up the majority of the class.

He said it was his opinion that the teacher just had a different way of teaching. I agreed, took my seat, and set out my class materials. I was flattered by the fact that he addressed me about this situation at all. I spent many more hours behind the closed door of our office, wanting to pull my hair out, trying to complete that course before it was done.

There were many projects I hadn't been able to complete and didn't want to bother with, that as the end of class came closer, I doubled down on, reworked, and resubmitted to the teacher for help. There were so many times I begged for Tyler's help and so many times I just wanted to sit and cry. I wish I could have, it probably would have relieved a little stress, but I still couldn't.

Once class was over and the time came that grades were posted, I put off getting online to see what kind of grade I'd ended up with. Of course, it's easy to put that kind of thing off when you have a hard time logging onto the college website in the first place and must have your teenager's help. Tyler patiently helped me log in and stood there, probably for moral support in case of a less than desirable outcome, while I was finally able to pull up my grade. There, looking back at me for the final grade in this class from hell, was an "A." I sat in silent disbelief for a moment before asking Tyler, "How the hell did that happen??"

"Mom," he said, "you went to class, did the projects, and turned them in. This is what happens when you do that."

I had, in fact, done those things, as well as participating a lot in class discussions and doing any extra credit offered. This was how I had gotten through many of my college courses. Still, I just couldn't believe what I was seeing on my computer screen at that moment. Too bad I am still computer illiterate. It just isn't my thing.

My best intentions didn't always work out, of course. There was that Spanish class I ended up dropping before it ended. I had never taken a class in a foreign language before. I really wanted to learn to speak Spanish, not only for my own personal growth but also for the advantage it would give me in my job. I was at a disadvantage from the get-go, as most of the other students had taken Spanish classes before and could speak the language, even if at a minimum. I fell further and further behind, just trying to catch up to their day one.

This was taking place during the holidays, and I was making my life more miserable with the stress I was adding to my already stressful life. Since taking this course was not a requirement, I decided (with Dave's help) to accept defeat and drop it. It really was such a relief.

Another time, during the most stressful class of my college career, statistics, I was again ready to throw in the towel. I was having such a hard time, even with the help of my tutor, and I longed for relief. One night, while at the home of the gentleman who tutored me through this statistics class and all my algebra classes, he was trying desperately to teach me something, and I was trying desperately to understand him. Finally, a wave of helplessness and hopelessness found its way into my soul. "I just can't do this anymore," I told him. "I just don't understand all this, and I don't believe I ever will."

I was too distraught to try to complete the steps he was trying to teach me that evening, and our time together ended with me packing up my books, along with my pride, and saying, "I think I'm going to have to give this class up."

He, in turn, said, "I will respect whatever decision you make, but I want you to know if you decide to finish it, I will do whatever I can to help you."

I went home and walked directly over to where Dave was sitting on the couch watching TV. I dropped to my knees in front of him, near tears, and told him, "I just can't get this statistics stuff anymore. I think I'm going to have to drop this class."

He let me unload my emotional baggage, quietly listening until I was finished. He then said, "You have to do what you think is best, and I cannot make that decision for you." He knew how much work I had put into all this and how many years I had been trying to achieve my goal of moving on to a four-year university.

He wasn't about to be the one to take the blame if I quit now. I don't blame him. Only I could make this decision. I couldn't bear the thought that all the work I had already put in and all the time it took me to do it would be for nothing if I quit now. Nor was the thought of yet another failure in my life appealing to me. I wanted to finish what I had started. So, I did. I reached out to my tutor, Don, and told him I had decided to complete this class and would like to take him up on his offer to help me. He was more than happy to oblige. We worked hard together, and at the end of the semester, I was proud to bring him home an "A" in statistics. Don and his wife, Timber, attended my graduation ceremony, both of them near tears.

Another time I slipped in strength, and tears overtook my determination to stay strong during those years when turmoil was the norm for my family and me, was when I read one of the many poems my brother wrote.

I'm not sure why I fought so long and hard against shedding a few tears, knowing how cleansing it was for the soul. You would think I would know that, having been moved to tears so easily and often when I was younger. I guess it was in trying to build more strength that I battled against it now and was usually successful in doing so.

This time was different, though, and I now believe that letting go of a few tears during the times you need to most is an even bigger strength than holding them in.

Chapter Thirty
Sunshine in Heaven

I clearly remember one of the first times in my adult life when I did not give in to tears in a situation where I normally would have. It was when someone I worked with came down on me for something I did or didn't do. It was when I'd gone back to waitressing after the Challenger disaster took place, and I, along with many others working in the space industry, was laid off.

When this person got upset with me, she scolded me in a condescending and somewhat intimidating manner. I really was taken aback. She looked like she wanted to spit (she was a little rough around the edges), and my eyes filled with tears; so stung was I from the look she gave me. It was then that I heard a stern voice come over my shoulder and threaten, "You cry, and I'll kill ya." Needless to say, I didn't cry.

My brother, Brian, has written numerous poems over the years, and his dear friend had gone through the grueling process of collecting, editing, and organizing them as she typed each one up. Even Brian did not realize how many he had written over the years. There was enough to fill three large binders. All the poems in one of those binders had been published into what is referred to as *Volume One* of three books. I had immediately bought a copy but put off reading it as I was concerned about getting back on that emotionally raw roller coaster ride he and our family had been riding on with him since he was nineteen and I was fourteen or fifteen. I needed time to prepare myself to visit the thoughts he had put on paper.

Evidently, I didn't wait long enough, as my reading came to a halt as I read a poem he'd written called "Sunshine in Heaven." I had, in fact, heard this poem before. He had read it to everyone present at our parents' 50th wedding anniversary party many years prior. Still, with Dad, Mom, and Barbara now gone, Brian currently being cared for in a healthcare facility, and me having gone through, and still going through, what cancer has dealt out to my family and me, it had a much more profound effect on me as I read it now.

A few of the verses pulled at my heart, almost bringing me to tears, but I pushed them aside, as I had been all my tears. That is until the end of the poem when Brian referred to "Sunshine in Heaven" I knew he was referring to Linda, and I could no longer contain the flood of feelings being held hostage in my heart.

I gave into the wave of grief that was sitting with me on the loveseat. There I was, curled up with my arms wrapped around my knees, sobbing. Tyler walked by a couple of times, and I'm not sure if he noticed that I was crying and said something to Dave or if Dave just happened by and saw me there. "What are you doing?" he asked.

"I'm crying," I said.

"Why?"

I explained Brian's poem to him. He, of course, consoled me as best he could. It was soothing enough to me for the time being; however, the impact of the words Brian had written in that poem had pulled me back in time and sat me back next to Barbara in the third and last seat of our station wagon as the family traveled through the miles of my youth.

With Dad being in the military, we had the opportunity to drive and see a lot of beautiful places. We spent three years in Germany and took many road trips there, pulling a pop-up tent trailer behind our station wagon and camping along the way. We also traveled across the United States a couple of times. Dad's family was from Massachusetts, and while that would be our destination upon leaving California, we visited and explored those states in between. My father absolutely loved to drive and took advantage of every opportunity to get behind the wheel. The trips to all those beautiful places around the countries inspired my love of nature and travel.

I could not stop reflecting on the feelings Brian's poem had stirred in me or my yearning to once again be that carefree child riding along in that car, even for just a moment. That is until I decided to do what works best for me and put my thoughts and feelings on paper. My poem titled "I didn't know" is the mirror of the emotions Brian's poem brought out in me. I will first share Brian's poem "Sunshine in Heaven" the way it appears in his book.

"Sunshine in Heaven"

I think of the times when we were young:
Dad driving the car, Mom leading the songs to be sung—
Six happy voices in unison, sounding so fine,
With Mom starting out, "You are my sunshine...."

261

The Luck of The Draw

I was just a small voice in the family chorus.
Not knowing the meaning, I just sang for us,
The words blending together, the singing in time,
The verses ever-changing, "my only sunshine…"

Dad wouldn't sing, but he'd drive—a happier man,
Listening to the voices of his family that God had planned.
I'd remember the words as we'd drive through the day,
"You make me happy when skies are gray…"

The journey was to my Grandma's, but the route was unclear,
And we knew a day of driving would get us there.
Dad was the driver. He always knew the way, too.
"You'll never know, dear, how much I love you…"

We were only seven with a song, on a trip,
Motoring through the land on an asphalt strip,
Singing songs while the miles rolled away,
"Please don't take my sunshine away…"

If time were miles, I'd drive in reverse,
To the place we were singing, knowing no hurt.
For our memories are not forgotten of when we were still seven.
Six of us still singing—the sunshine in heaven.

Brian K. Fraser

March 25, 1992

"I Didn't Know"

I didn't know I would cry that day,
Especially in light of the years I had kept those tears at bay.

But when I woke that morning, I didn't know about the poem I would read,
He wrote about the car that carried seven, one of whom was me.

With Dad at the wheel, we traveled many miles together,
Seeing the beautiful world under the watchful eye of our mother.

Five kids filled the backseats and did their best to behave,
During the hours it took to reach whatever destination lay at the end of each day.

Sunshine in Heaven

Still, kids will be kids, and we sometimes pushed our luck,
To the point that Dad pulled over, and then his quiet words loudly stuck.

With the car back in motion, we continued happily along,
'Til the day the car stalled, and our journey went terribly wrong.

We didn't see it coming, and we'll never understand why,
God decided one must leave us without ever even saying goodbye.

Through the crushing pain, Dad asked the Lord, "How can I even drive,
In this car when I know my second-born daughter is no longer alive?"

God leaned in through the window and said, "I know it hurts that she's gone,
But the six of you have many more miles to travel still, and you must move on.

So, Dad started the engine and followed his faith,
Down a road he hoped would take the rest of his family to a happier place.

There have been many more bumps for us all on this rugged road, which we call life,
Our mother lost her husband, and soon thereafter, we kids lost his wife.

The author of the poem I read on the day of which I speak,
Is our brother, who has suffered terribly since the void was left in that back seat.

We siblings too soon said goodbye to another, and there again we mourned,
As one more sister passed to keep company with the parents to whom she was born.

So, when he spoke of "Sunshine in Heaven," I knew just who he meant,
It was the angel who had her wings clipped much too soon after she'd been sent.

So, I cried not just because he hurt in that way,
I cried for the hurt we all felt when we drove off without her on that day.

Sandra R. Pickles

November 25, 2021

I also thought of my determination when dealing with the eye surgery my eye doctor told me was a must in 2022. I had developed cataracts in both eyes, which had been brought about by a combination of the cancer, steroids, and other medications I was on. My eye doctor told me I probably shouldn't even be driving. Cataract surgery became a must, and I couldn't schedule it fast enough.

The eye doctor needed authorization from my oncologist to perform the surgery. He let me know that his office would contact the cancer center and have a discussion with him or his nurse, asking that they provide his office with written approval to perform the surgery.

My oncologist said eye surgery would be fine, but it would need to be done during the week off from my chemo infusions. Fair enough. I could only have one eye done at a time, which meant a month between surgeries.

After having an appointment with the surgeon who would perform the surgery, I had an appointment over the phone with the person in charge of scheduling surgery. She would set up the first surgery and provide me with all the details of what to do before and after the procedure. I got out the little calendar book that had my treatment schedule mapped out. I determined when my week off would be and set up my first appointment in March. I couldn't wait.

Unbeknownst to me at the time, I made an error in calculating my week off. Mistakes like this are the norm for me, and it constantly causes issues in the household and in the progress of my trying to build back my self-confidence. The week before what would have been the first of the two surgeries, I looked at the calendar and realized I was scheduled for infusions the same week I had planned my eye surgery. I immediately called the young lady with whom I'd made the appointment and explained the situation. "Can I reschedule for the following week?"

Unfortunately, there were no openings in the month of April, so I was scheduled for the first week in May. *Damn, another six weeks out.* I was driving to Santa Barbara once a week for other treatments, and the blurred vision was a concern for me.

What was even more distressing was that I had used the calculations of my week off to make arrangements with two friends to come to California to visit me for a couple of days in July, during what I thought would be my week off, but now, of course, wouldn't be. They both had already scheduled time off work. One was flying in from Tennessee and already had flight reservations. The other was coming from the Sacramento area and already had her train ticket. I did not want to have them change things up, so I asked the nurse in the infusion room to pass a message on to my doctor, who I would not see for another three weeks or more, if a solution could be considered allowing me that week in July off. She promised to pass on the message.

Mind you, these two friends and I had previously planned a trip to Costa Rica together, and we had a week booked at an all-inclusive resort there scheduled for March 5th through March 12th. I made these reservations sometime in May 2021, and we already had the resort paid in full. We were on pins and needles, waiting for the time to come. I had not seen Kim, my high school friend from Tennessee, in over nineteen years. Upon getting the news in December 2021 of the need to go on chemo and the timetable for treatments that would be required, along with the concern of my immune system being weakened even more, I had to reconsider if this trip was safe for me.

We are still living with the pandemic and severe issues at airports and with air passengers, along with flight cancelations. There was also the concern of stories about American citizens' safety in Costa Rica. Between the three of us, we decided it would be best to cancel the trip and stay in the United States. It was so disappointing. We considered meeting at an Air B&B in another state, but they then decided it would be best to keep me out of airports and off airplanes altogether, so the plan was made for the two of them to come to my home for a couple of days. I certainly did not want to have to cancel this gathering, too.

I explained all of this to my oncologist, saying there was no way I could miss out on my plans. We would eventually alter my infusion schedule to make it work, which again is not easy because of the timetables needing to be approved by my insurance carrier.

As fate would have it, the week delay in treatment turned into a two-week delay because I tested positive for Covid. I later had a hell of a time getting my treatments back on track for Mondays and Tuesdays rather than the Wednesdays and Thursdays the center now had me scheduled for. It took some effort from the center's scheduler to make that magic happen, but thankfully, it did.

My friends and I did spend a few happy days together that turned all those hassles into distant memories.

I recall a time when Kim was living with us in California, before we moved to Florida, when she and I jumped into her Ford Pinto and headed off to Los Angeles for a weekend without clearing it with my parents. For that matter, we didn't even bother waiting for them to get off work to tell them we were going in the first place. I knew I was in trouble before we left. Still, I was eighteen. How much trouble could I really be in?

I can't recall what the consequences were when we returned home from our little adventure. All I remember was how excited I was that we had no idea where we were going, where we would end up or stay when we got there. Kim had some distant cousins that lived in LA and thought she could find their home without directions. We never did find them, but we sure did have a good time trying.

What about that time too, when I was eighteen and anxious to fly the coop? Kim and I planned to move to her parents' home in Florida once she finished the classes required to complete her high school credentials. Being one year ahead of her in school, I had already graduated some ten months before her finishing up her classes.

Her father, like mine, was in the Air Force and had just retired. Her parents were having a home built in Punta Gorda, Florida, and they wanted her to join them. Kim lived with my family while she completed school, as her parents were already in Florida, overseeing the construction of their new home. They lived in a condominium during the building.

It was simply a given that we couldn't be separated, and being that I would be going into a safe home with her parents, it made for the perfect opportunity to leave the town I couldn't wait to get away from. Kim and I were both so excited and counted down the days. My father was not so enthusiastic. Not only was I the last of five children, but I was also the only daughter to move out from under his roof without being married. As any dad would be, he was concerned.

Before leaving California, Kim and I had driven to Santa Rosa, California, in my cool car, so we could attend the wedding of one of my cousins. Many of my mother's family members were there, and it was a great opportunity to see them all before my big move. Our plan was to head to Florida from there. We were all packed up and saying our goodbyes. Family members stood in the driveway next to the car, bidding us farewell and wishing us a safe trip. The problem was, Dad couldn't say goodbye. For that matter, he couldn't seem to talk at all.

My father had been very strict with all of us kids growing up, and it caused me to resent him many times over many years. Often, Kim and I were both angry with his overprotective ways, and we spent much more time at her house than we did mine. Her parents were much more lenient with us. On this day, though, things were different. Kim and I were both so choked up over him being so emotionally torn and unable to speak that we both started crying. We pulled out of that driveway and cried all the way to San Francisco, which is about fifty miles south of Santa Rosa.

We were, though, so excited to be on our way to our new destination in life. We drove some three thousand miles across the states, with me behind the wheel the entire time. It took us about five days to get there. We had a great time there for a while, though I only ended up living in Florida for a short time. I was back home in California before Christmas that year.

Many years later, out of the clear blue sky, my father would tell me that I was his brave one. We were standing in our living room when he said it, and I remember looking at him and thinking, "Who are you, and what did you do with my father?"

I asked him what it was that made him say that, and he answered, "You were the only daughter who was single and left home to strike out on your own."

That thought had never occurred to me, and I was flattered. After all, Dad didn't give out many compliments in those days.

Chapter Thirty-One
Silver Lining in Every Cloud

So, back to the day my doctor advised me to schedule a consultation for Car-T therapy, and we left his office. A foreboding silence hung between Dave and me at the start of the drive home, and I wondered if, at this very moment, like me, he was already reliving those days from hell that we had endured in that hotel room up north during and after my stem cell transplant in 2018. How I hated that my cancer was once again putting more pressure on us. Especially him.

My concern over what this has done to me does not hold a candle to my concern over what it has done to my family. I am at least aware of how I am feeling mentally and physically, and I usually have some control over how I react or what I need to do to get through the trying moments. When it comes to others, though, not only do I not know when or what they are or are not thinking about the situation, but I also cannot experience their reactions to their thoughts and fears or how they get themselves through their moments. How do I know when they need to be consoled?

I am thankful my father did not live long enough to learn about my diagnosis. During his later years, he spent a lot of time worrying about his wife and children. Especially during the last few months of his life while he was in a healthcare facility. There was little more for him to do there than lie in a bed and think as he tried to defy death. His attitude differed greatly from our mother's almost nonchalant attitude toward dying.

Mom had spent years volunteering at an old folks' home, where she would style hair for women who couldn't do it themselves. She knew how much better it made them feel to look their best. She saw and heard first-hand the suffering people go through when they are simply sick and tired of being sick and tired and are waiting to go. Mom shared some stories with me about those little ladies. One particularly disheartening one for her was when she was doing one of these little ladies' hair, and the woman cried out, with no warning whatsoever, "I want to die, I just want to die." That's how unhappy she was, waiting and wanting her next breath to be her last.

While taking a speech class during my college years, one of the subjects I chose to speak on was that of Dr. Kevorkian, aka "Dr. Death." The gist of the speech was, "while I am not a fan of expediting someone's demise, people should have the right to choose to die with dignity." Especially if they are suffering terribly, with no hope for a cure or comeback from whatever is ailing them. I feel we show more mercy to our pets when we put them into a restful sleep when it's their time, and I believe we should show people the same respect.

So, as I sat stewing in anger and self-pity at the thought of having to once again live through the experience I'd already lived through during those dark days up north, some of which I still can't account for, when I suddenly had an epiphany. "Wait," I thought, "…no, really … wait. What if this procedure really worked and gave me more remission time than the stem cell transplant had? What if I didn't have to have Dave drive me to the cancer center on Mondays and Tuesdays for three weeks on and one week off, where he then had to sit in the parking lot waiting for me for two-plus hours every time? What if I could get off the chemo that was poisoning me, as well as those damn steroids I had to take every Monday?" which drove me nuts and caused way more than its fair share of tiffs between Dave and me due to the negative impact it had on my mood.

"Oh, and what about those blood draws I wouldn't have to have early every Monday morning on those weeks I was scheduled for treatment? What would it be like to feel like my life belonged to me rather than to the cancer that dictated our schedules and our way of life? We could even start doing some real traveling after my recovery!!"

Yes, I knew I would be going to hell and back again, but the keywords here were "back again," and in that moment, I couldn't get to hell fast enough. All I could think of now was getting home and opening my laptop, so I could start researching those hospitals within a reasonable distance that offered this procedure and who had the doctor best qualified to do it. I already knew I didn't want to go back to the hospital up north. I couldn't get past the bad taste in my mouth from the experience we'd already had there.

Before I had this epiphany, the subject that also came up during the drive home was the alternative treatments I had been undergoing and the faith I had put into them. Based on these new circumstances, Dave now had more ammunition in his argument against them, and even I had to admit they were not producing the results I'd been hoping for. So, I agreed to throw in the towel, go off the diet I had been following, and back off from the treatments I was having down south.

I kept the appointments I had already scheduled with those doctors, got my last treatments in, and explained to them why I would be holding off on returning for a while. After not having these services for a while, I needed to see what my numbers would do and then use those results as a measuring stick to gauge their effectiveness.

Both doctors were, of course, disappointed to hear of the changes in my health and tried to persuade me to continue with the treatments they were providing. They said these things do take time to make a difference. I explained that I felt doing so would be like continually buying clothes I knew didn't fit me. I just couldn't see the sense in putting time, money, and effort into something that didn't seem to be making a difference.

"My numbers are actually going up," I said to both of them, "rather than going down. Or, for that matter, even staying the same."

I'm not saying I don't have faith in integrative medicine because I really do. I just couldn't justify their use for me at that moment. They understood and wished me well with the new therapy I would be undergoing, hopefully sooner rather than later.

My research of facilities offering what we were looking for led me to a hospital down south about half the distance from the one we'd gone to up north. I was thrilled to read about a doctor there who specializes in my type of cancer, and from the sounds of the reviews I was reading, she had an impeccable reputation. My research ended there. It was the first and only place I'd looked at, and I called the facility to make an appointment after discussing it with Dave.

I can't tell you how impressed we were to get a call back from this doctor's assistant soon after calling the new patient line and making my needs known to the representative that answered the phone. Even more impressive was how soon they were able to schedule us for a consultation with the doctor. I was beyond excited this was all happening. There are no words that can explain my longing for some sign of hope for remission after all the physical and emotional trauma this disease had caused me and those close to me over the past five years. I prayed that this was that sign.

Our first consultation with this new doctor of mine took place early in June 2022 at a facility different from the one where I would be treated going forward. It was quite some distance from our home. The hospital's social worker made reservations for us for an overnight stay at a nearby hotel offering their patients discounted rates. We counted down the days and did our best to make the time away from home a little adventure. This facility is in the heart of one of California's most beautiful oceanside cities. We treated ourselves to a nice dinner in the harbor, enjoying a sunset view as we dined.

The following day, we packed our belongings, checked out of the hotel, and headed to my appointment. The meeting with my doctor and her assistant was bittersweet, as once again, I was reminded of just how precarious my health is. After studying my chart, this doctor told me she was adding me to the list of patients waiting for Car-T therapy as an urgent candidate. She explained it would take anywhere between three to six months for me to be called in just to have my white blood cells extracted from my body for their use in this therapy. After collection, it would be another six to eight weeks before I was scheduled for the chemo treatments I would need.

After that, those cells would be infused back into my body. By then, they would have been genetically engineered to seek out and kill the cancer cells. Unfortunately, they will also kill off some of my good cells. She warned us of the possible long, and short-term side effects of this procedure and the drugs that would be used. What do you do, though?? I wanted this done, like yesterday.

She also talked about choosing clinical trials rather than the therapy we were currently discussing, which had already been FDA-approved. We opted out of that option.

As usual, the information we were given was overwhelming, and trying to follow the train of thought of those experts providing us with these details was next to impossible. We left that meeting in a mood more somber than when we first entered. The thought most unsettling for me by this time was that maybe it wasn't just the devil trying to wipe me off the face of this earth. I couldn't help but wonder now if God wasn't on board with him, too.

Why is he trying so hard to remove me from this planet? I wondered. I have a list of inspirational quotes saved on my laptop that I read in the mornings from time to time, and two of those that I am especially fond of are:

1. I belong here, and I deserve to take up space.
2. There is room for me at the table.

While I honestly have faith in God, I think even those most loyal to Him sometimes waiver in their belief. I must admit that mine was beginning to fade a bit at this point. Was I not important enough even to Him to take up space here? Did He no longer have room left for me at the table?

I thought of the expensive dinner Dave and I had treated ourselves to the night before. I had felt guilty about how much money we'd spent since I am usually so frugal, remembering those years when my income was below the poverty level. I told Dave that going forward, I planned to enjoy life more, even if it cost more, and not feel bad about it. Since we seemed to be getting bad news on a regular basis now related to my health, I felt that I probably had less time to live and that I should take every opportunity I could to enjoy life while I was still here.

The fact that the doctor was so concerned about my health that she put me on that waiting list as an urgent candidate, after just a few short minutes of reviewing my bloodwork and medical records, fed my worst fears.

We got in the car and prepared ourselves for the drive home. After driving in silence for a bit, I turned to Dave and said, "Honey, I really need you to be positive for me now."

His response was his usual, "Yeah, right!!"

I can typically turn my attitude around when I'm sad or scared; that's just my nature. Unfortunately, it is not Dave's. He doesn't look to find the silver lining in things.

Often when people remark on how amazed they are at how positive and happy I always seem to be, I jokingly tell them I have to be to make up for Dave's lack thereof. I realize I need to understand that that's just his way. We are who we are. Still, I needed a little help with my own thoughts and fears at the moment, and I needed him to know that. "Please, try to provide me with some positive vibes." I reminded him I was at least now on the list with those waiting for this procedure, and hopefully, I would get it done sooner rather than later. I wanted him to take as much solace in that as I was trying to.

Back in January, a friend of ours called me to offer her support when I was so upset after learning of my new chemo treatments. This person was dealing with cancer herself, and not for the first time. I had told her that there was almost always a silver lining in every cloud and that I am the kind of person who would find the one in this one. I told her I appreciated her call and knowing I could reach out to her whenever I needed to. I later sent her a thank-you card, telling her how much I appreciated her phone call and concern.

Chapter Thirty-Two
Welcome to Fiji

Our appointment with the doctor down south had ended with the understanding that she would be in touch with my local oncologist to plan what to do about my disease between now and when the Car-T therapy could take place.

Though she and my regular oncologist were unable to communicate before my next regularly scheduled monthly appointment with him, he confirmed that I would need something more to keep the cancer in check while waiting for my name to be called off that list of candidates. Later, these two doctors would decide that I would need to take an oral form of chemo on top of the infusions I was already getting. Out of curiosity, we asked my oncologist if this would cause my hair to fall out. He said it probably would. We just weren't sure when.

A request to fill this new prescription was provided to the specialty pharmacy we go through, and I went to pick it up. There was some confusion about how to handle and take this medication, and I spoke several times with one of the nurses I sometimes saw in place of my regular oncologist. She asked that I bring the medication in with me on treatment day and its instructions so she could go over it with me before I took it. In the pamphlet that comes with medications, you know, the one that lists all those wonderful side effects these meds may have, I noticed it said not to handle this medication unless you're wearing gloves. *Wait ... what?? Are you serious?* This shit my doctors prescribed me is so toxic that it's not safe for me to hold it in the palm of my hand, yet they want me to ingest it? Wow!! I felt another one of those stinging sensations in my eyes. I tell Dave this, and of course, it upsets him too. Nonetheless, he makes sure I have a pair of gloves to take with me to treatment.

I call and let the nurse know I'm on my way, and she promises to meet me in the infusion room. True to her word, she comes in and over to the chair I'm waiting in to be hooked up for my infusion. She kneels down by my side so she can be at eye level with me as we speak, and I share with her what the instructions say about gloves. She says she doesn't think I really have to worry about putting them on when handling the medication. I show her the instructions, and after reading them, she says, while it wouldn't be safe, say, for her to handle these pills without gloves on, it's okay for me to.

Wow, how's that for making a person feel less important than the next? I knew it wasn't her intent to make me feel this way. She was, in fact, doing her best to console me; still, that's how I felt. Damn, if that stinging sensation didn't make its way back to my eyes, as once again, I fought back the tears.

I begrudgingly counted out the ten pills the weekly dosage calls for and swallowed them. It was not a happy day for me—another of those tougher ones that I have no choice but to push through.

I am still on these pills, and yes, my hair is falling out, so much so that it is thin and unsightly. I often find it in the sink when I brush it and in my food when I'm eating. I go and have it cut short to try to alleviate some of this, and I'm happy with the look of my short and sassy haircut.

While waiting my turn to be next in line for the procedure I am hoping will put me into remission, I have a phone conversation with the gal who'd had a stem cell transplant up north at the same time I did. We had been keeping in touch over the years, and she'd had several other health issues during that time. Now, since her cancer had come back some time ago, the same as mine had, her doctor had recommended she have the same Car-T therapy I was waiting to have. She told me she hadn't even confirmed with him that she wanted to do this before finding out that he had her scheduled to start the process on the 8th of August. Geez. Here I was, an urgent candidate, still waiting for a call to say it was my turn to get started with this, and she got scheduled for it without even asking. I'm really happy for her and wish her all the best. Still, I'm a little envious too.

Some time passed, and I was anxious to find out how things were going for her with the procedure. I called her in early August, knowing the time for her cell collection was coming soon.

It turned out she was in the hospital waiting on this and getting help for some of those other health issues she'd been dealing with. She sounded so exhausted and was having difficulty carrying on an intelligible conversation with me. This was so disheartening. Usually, when my friend and I talk, I can barely keep up with her while trying to get a word in myself. Now, though, I suggested she rest and told her to call me when she is feeling better. She agreed a different time to talk would be better for her, and we ended our conversation. It was hard for me not to be shaken after we hung up, and I shared her situation and our conversation with Dave. "She sounded pretty bad," I told him.

A couple of weeks later, I sent her a text, asking if she had had her cells collected and, if so, how things went. I did not get an answer. Remembering how tired she sounded the last time we talked and reminding myself of the other things she was dealing with, I decided to hold off a while on texting her.

In October, I texted her again, letting her know my cell collection was scheduled for the 26th of the month, and told her how excited I was to start this. I asked how she was doing. No answer. I began to feel uneasy. A sense of a Déjà vu was settling inside my soul from the previous experience I'd had when trying to check in with my coworker, who had been in the process of getting her second stem cell transplant, when I was made aware of her unfortunate passing. Maybe subconsciously, I chose to try to remain in denial that there could be anything seriously wrong going on with this person now too, and I put off calling her.

One night at the end of November, I was in bed, drifting off to sleep. Since I have such a hard time getting and staying asleep, I usually turn my cell phone off before laying it next to me on the nightstand. I heard it vibrate this night, and I was a little irritated that someone was texting me so late. I did not check my phone.

The next morning, as I sat having my quiet time, I checked my messages to see who had texted me so late the night before. On it was an answer to the last text message I had sent to my friend. It came over under her name, but the message was not from her. It came from her son. In this text, he said he didn't check his mom's phone often but had just noticed I had tried to text her some time back. He told me his mom passed away in August, and he just wanted to inform me of that, so I didn't think she was ignoring me. He said he was sorry about giving me bad news at this hour and really hoped I had a great rest of my night.

I dropped my head to rest on my knees and cupped my face in my hands, shaking my head back and forth, screaming silently, "Dear God, no! This just can't be!"

Yet, I knew it was.

I sent my condolences to my friend's son, thanking him for letting me know of this. I remember meeting him at the hospital when his mother and I had our stem cell transplants, and I reminded him of what a wonderful person she was.

I was shaken. Here I was, so excited to get started with the same procedure my friend was in the process of having done when she passed. I don't know if she even made it out of the hospital, and I wouldn't feel right asking her son for details. I was unsure if I wanted to tell Dave, but I did.

I reminded myself that while this person was battling the same disease I am when she was undergoing or preparing to undergo the same procedure I am anxiously waiting on, she had some other health issues going on, too. I try to continue believing I'm going to be all right and that everything will work out fine. Still, it's getting harder and harder for me to keep the faith. My friend had a lot of confidence in God, too, and talked to me about it every time we spoke. I do my best to follow her example as I continue believing and praying for the best.

As we waited anxiously for the call that would tell us that I was next on the list for this procedure, we were concerned about a group trip to Fiji that we were a part of. The group going included six members of the Pickles family. We had booked this trip long before covid hit, and it had been postponed several times due to shutdowns and travel restrictions. We got word that it would for sure be a go in mid-October. Flights were in the process of being booked by the young lady hosting the group. When she called me for information on our passports, I told her we might have to cancel the trip since I couldn't chance missing my place on the treatment list if we got called. She tried to see if another couple could go, but they couldn't.

She and I both agreed that we should book our flights and hope for the best. I sent her our passport information but didn't tell Dave at the time since he and I had decided some time back that it would be safer for me if we stayed home. I didn't want to stress him out, so I waited a while before sharing this. I told my sister-in-law, Lisa, though, and after a few drinks while at our nephew's wedding, we nonchalantly broke the news to him. The next day, he said, "So, I hear we are going to Fiji?"

I don't think he even remembered who told him. Well, it was an open bar at the reception. I was like, "Well … yeah," like this was old news that I expected him to already know.

I will say someone was looking out for me. During the first week of October, an email came in from my doctor's coordinator, saying I was to go off all medications on the 10th of October, as I was scheduled for my cell collection on the 26th of October.

We were scheduled to leave for Fiji on Thursday the 13th and would return home on Saturday the 22nd. We would then go Tuesday the 25th to make my appointment down south. How's that for all the stars aligning? It was almost like I'd made the phone call to the hospital myself and told them I needed the exact schedule they had given me. I couldn't wait to share my good news with the rest of the family members. When I did, they were as ecstatic as I was. We had a great trip. I was so thankful to have had this wonderful experience before starting my treatments.

Soon after my cell collection, various other appointments were scheduled for me in preparation for cell therapy. I would need a PET scan, brain scan, a bone marrow biopsy, more blood work, and three chemo infusions before my cells would be returned to my body. All these appointments were scheduled in December, except for the last chemo infusion, which would take place on the 1st of January, 2023. I would then be given a two-day break, and on the 4th of January, my cells, which would have been engineered to seek out and kill the cancer cells in my body, would be given back to me.

Hotel reservations were made for us at the hospital's hotel facilities for all these appointments. Once the chemo infusions started, we would be there for close to a month. We are beyond thrilled that this is all really happening now. Friends and family are as excited as I am when I share this information with them, and I am counting down the days.

Chapter Thirty-Three
Permanent Resident

I am of an age that I know what it's like to want something so bad you feel you can taste it. I've experienced that sensation several times. I spoke earlier about losing my sister when I was eleven, and I learned at a level no one should have to at that age what it's like to try to will someone to walk through the front door of the house, just once more, the same way they had a hundred times before. Death is, of course, so permanent.

I try not to visit too intimately with the memories of some of the dreams I had as a child, whose first experience with death was losing one of her beloved siblings. Some of those dreams, however, remain as clear to me as the images of my mother when she fainted during services being held for her daughter. Those will be branded in my brain for life. The first time she fainted was at the service held for Linda on the air force base we lived on. My parents stood next to my sister's casket, my mother leaning against my father's chest as he stood behind her. Thank God he was behind her and felt her go limp and start sliding down his body. He was able to hold and support her, preventing her from slipping out of his embrace.

The gentleman from the mortuary was by their side almost instantly, pulling out a little vial that held a tiny wisp of sponge soaked with smelling salt. I watched her eyelashes flutter as she came to. It was amazing to me how quickly that smelling salt revived her. The second time was after services were spoken at the grounds of the cemetery in Santa Rosa, where Linda is buried. This time, though, she did not have my father standing behind her when I watched her eyes roll back into her head as she fainted and went down again. He was at her side, however, holding her arm and shoulder with both hands and easing her descent to the ground. Once she was laid comfortably across the grass, the gentleman from the mortuary was, once again, instantly by her side, waving the vile of smelling salt under her nose. I again watched her eyelashes flutter, marveling once more at how quickly it brought her back around.

There are times when these memories do visit, and I'm taken back to the morning after Linda's passing when we kids had no choice but to hear our mother's agony as she lay in her bed mourning. Her grief crawled up her gut, leaving her throat in screams I would later learn my sister Barbara described as those of a wild animal. Even with both our bedroom doors closed, the sound of her screams penetrated the wood, shattering both doors into splinters that pierced my ears, then my heart, and then on into my soul, where they're embedded still.

I have no idea how the family living at 524 Gum Street survived this period of time. So many kind friends and neighbors brought food to the house. Many times, dishes were left at the doorstep, and much of it went uneaten. I learned very young that you can go days without an appetite or even thinking of food and how foreign your appetite and food feel on an empty stomach once it returns.

The sense of sadness hung so heavy in our home during that time that my mother would later say that even our little dog, Penny, knew something was wrong with her people. She felt out of place alongside our emotions as she quietly lingered in the background of our pain. Our parents moved like zombies through the necessary preparations of burying their 17-year-old daughter. Rather than helping her pick out clothes for her graduation, they were instead searching her closet, trying to make a decision on which one of her dresses she should be buried in.

We three younger kids had not been allowed to see Linda after her passing. Our parents wanted us to remember her as she was when she was alive. Today I am thankful for the choice they made, as the picture framing my last memory of her holds that of a young girl excited to leave the house and be on her way to a beach party, where she would spend the day with her friends, and a boy, who was most likely her first real love interest.

She had been so impatient to get on the road, and I remember my father holding her up in the driveway of our house. I glanced out the window, seeing him leaning into the driver's side of the car as he ensured her seatbelt was fastened and gave her final safety instructions. He also reiterated the rule that she was not to drive off base. She promised she wouldn't, but unfortunately, she did not keep that promise, and leaving the base would lead to her accident.

It wasn't too many years later that the big brother I idolized fell ill, and it was I who answered the phone that evening when a stranger called to let my dad know he'd been taken to a hospital. His illness is not one that can be bandaged up and healed. I live with a longing every day that begs God for mercy in ending the nightmare that his life and that of our family's lives became after that call came through that night.

When I was 19, I was briefly treated for depression, but with some counseling, medication, and the support of my strong family, I was able to push through it. Though it only lasted a few months, it felt like a lifetime to me. I can honestly say in those days, I had little to no desire to go on.

During one of my darkest hours, my mother sat next to me as I lay in bed, crying, and tried to convince me that even with all she had been through in her life, she was glad to be alive and that being a mother was one of her most fulfilling roles in life. I told her I didn't want children, as I never wanted to experience the pain I watched her go through as a mother. Nor did I want to be responsible for bringing someone into the world who might also suffer as I had from those things that life throws out at us. She told me that if I were to never have a child, I would be missing out on one of the best experiences a woman can have in her lifetime. That of bringing a life into this world and the love I would always feel for that person. She said even after having four babies, it wasn't until after having me, her fifth, that she could honestly say she didn't want any more. How it must have broken her heart to hear me say between sobs, "God, Mom, I wish you would have stopped at four."

It amazes me when I think back to the feeling of not wanting to go on then and compare it to my insatiable desire to do everything I can to survive now.

In my adult life, the longings I had usually had to do with past love relationships I wished would work out, but were not meant to, so didn't. Others were positions I applied for at work, wishing so hard on the star I chose to make it all come true that when it didn't, it seemed like every star fell down from the sky. I know this is par for the course in life and that most people will, or have already experienced it in theirs.

The longing I can taste now and fall victim to at any given moment is one of a completely different and potentially all-consuming nature. It is that longing for a solution that can ease the thoughts that can come on as a sudden panic attack if I allow the truth about my condition to sink too deep into my mind. That truth being that I do, in fact, have an illness that has no cure. You know, that one the magazine article I read said is always fatal. The same disease listed as the cause of death on my brother-in-law's death certificate. The same one my friend and coworker, who had been scheduled for a second stem cell transplant, believing it would be as successful as the first one, which had extended her life some ten or twelve years, but instead, led to her passing, despite her prayers and best-fed beliefs. The same disease another friend of mine was fighting when she passed in August. Not to mention she was in the process of undergoing the same procedure I am anxiously waiting for. Oh, and let's not forget the part it played in my mother's passing, lessening her chances of surviving any medical procedures available to the doctors that could have tried to help her heal from the multitude of issues she was experiencing when she stroked.

As you may imagine, these panic attacks, brought on by the reality that you may soon lose your life, can be physically and emotionally crippling. They can suck the breath from your lungs and cause your body to feel hot one moment, turning that heat into cold sweats the next. The contemplation can be overwhelming. Even the line "if I should die before I wake," which I have said for years in my prayers before bed, took on a whole new meaning for me. I do, though, still recite that prayer every night before turning in.

While I have only experienced attacks to this degree a few times, I have had to accept the reality behind their cause and have had to, in some ways, come to terms with them.

289

There is also envy. It can come in a form as casual as being part of a conversation that takes place about goals that other people are in pursuit of. I think of those young adults sharing their excitement in their work and educational endeavors, and I think to myself that while others in the conversation may see the dreams of those individuals come to fruition one day, I may be the only one who is part of the conversation who may not. It is sad to me, as I am so taken with seeing dreams come true for people, and I'd like to think that I can witness their success along with those others.

I assume there will come a day when this disease takes its toll and wraps up the job it set out to do. I say "assume" since there are so many ways in which life could end for any of us. Only God knows when that time will come and what the cause will be. For now, I have no desire to know. I only know I want to live life in a way I can enjoy and be proud of. Yes, I have a disease, but I am not the disease itself. I want to appreciate every moment that I am here, and while I may not go willingly when my time comes, I do hope to go graciously.

I truly believe that gratitude is what brings us the most happiness in life. Even on the worst of days, I am thankful for the things I do have. To fill any "gap" I come across in my life, I use the following:

Gratitude

Attitude

Perseverance

I am loyal to my morning ritual of quiet time with God and my coffee. These moments are what I depend on to get me through life. Wondering what the day may hold is more than an exciting concept for me. Looking out the window as God wakes up the world brings me to life every time. Many are the moments when I am having a bad day or am sad about something, and I glance out our front window just in time to witness beautiful birds bathing in and drinking from the water fountain there. I can't recall even once that this has not brought me back to feeling joy and reignited my love for life in the moment. After coffee, I take a walk with Smokey, who is beyond excited to go outside, where I admire and appreciate the beautiful world in which we live.

In my life before cancer, there were many times I wondered how I would feel or react if I ever found out I had this disease. I remember one day years ago wondering this very thing and asking myself, "How do you know you don't already have it?" My years of dieting, consuming low-fat and fat-free foods ladened with sweeteners worse for you than regular sugar, had sometimes concerned me. I saw those warnings on every packet of artificial sweeteners I added to my coffee, tea, and cereals. That one that indicated that this product had been known to cause cancer in laboratory rats, and still, I used them, thinking, like most of us do, that cancer only ever happens to other people.

I was also aware of the dangers of smoking, yet I knowingly put my health at risk every time I lit and smoked a cigarette. I mean … really? Every one of those cigarette packs had a warning label on them, similar to those artificial sweetener packets that said, "This product has been known to cause cancer." Still, I allowed my addiction to override any health concerns and smoked for some sixteen years. I continuously dieted, desperate to fit in with the standards society sets for women.

While I do have a lot of resentment that this life-threatening disease came about in this body of mine, especially when I worked so hard to live a healthy lifestyle at the time it did, this uninvited guest has opened my eyes in many joyous ways too. Do I wish I didn't have it? Of course! Still, there are some positive changes that came about in my life and in me as a person because of it, and I am thankful for them.

Life and everything in it is even more precious to me now. Even though it was before, too, I now have a heightened sense of euphoria in living and loving, wanting to drink in every emotion and every detail I experience throughout my every day and every night.

My senses are heightened, making the sky bluer, the grass greener, every smell is sweeter (well, most of them), and life is much more precious to me. I love deeper and am more willing and anxious to share these emotions with as many of those as I can. I want the best for others, and nothing makes me happier than making someone else's day.

I've also learned how important it is to treat myself better and practice self-care regularly. Before being diagnosed, I didn't take much time to do that. I felt guilty about spending time or money on myself at all. I would rather be doing those things for somebody else.

My cancer, of course, can no longer be considered an uninvited guest that will eventually go home. It is a permanent resident in this body of mine and our household since there is no cure for multiple myeloma at this time. Hopefully, one day there will be. Until that day, though, we must live together as harmoniously as possible. Yes, we fight and disagree. I can't always conceal my rage against it or the unwanted pain and side effects it has brought to me, those I love, and those who love me back. Cancer has dimmed my expectations of living into my eighties as my parents did. You never know, though. I continuously pray for a long-lasting maintenance plan or, of course, a cure.

Chapter Thirty-Four
Moving Forward

As I hang tight now to the hope that this therapy will be the answer to my prayers and my survival, I pray that I am not putting too much faith into it and setting myself up for disappointment yet again. Especially when I don't know what would be available to me next if it doesn't work. For now, I can only do my best to think positively and prepare myself mentally and physically for the upcoming procedure.

In the time between now and then, I must keep my mind busy. Since I require more sleep now than I had in the past, I have learned to be even more appreciative of my waking hours. It is important to me that I use them wisely and be as productive as possible. I have set many goals. Finishing this book is the biggest one at this time.

I talked about procrastinating on homework in high school, where I would be docked at least five points for turning assignments in late. In my college days, that habit went into reverse. It seemed such a struggle to keep up with what I was trying to learn that I would sometimes read through the material for the following week's classes, so I might have an advantage later.

As an adult, putting off doing homework caused me more stress than the work itself did. The only way I could relieve that pressure was to be working on whatever assignment was due next. I drug my bag of homework with me everywhere, even when I knew there was no chance of my getting to it. That bag became my security blanket. If something was due on a Wednesday night, I wanted it completed and ready to be handed in no later than Monday night. There had to be that day in between for "what-ifs." What if I didn't work on it until the night before it was due, that there was something I didn't understand or couldn't get through? What if I or someone in my family got sick, or something unexpected came up Tuesday, and I couldn't finish it at the last minute? What if I found out I'd done it wrong and would now need time to fix it? So, my bad habit of putting off schoolwork was something I was successful in overcoming.

Never would I ever have thought, though, that my deadline to get a project done would be one where I was trying to outlive the possibility that I may pass before it was completed. This book has become that project. I wish to finish strong, and soon, as it is true what Dave says, he cannot finish it for me.

When I look back on my college career, where I worked hard, stressing out to complete and turn in my homework, along with other required projects, on time, I feel I owe it to myself and Dave to do the best I can to finish up our story. I would love to be that one student I dreamed of being by getting this all wrapped up on the deadline I had set in my mind long ago.

What one student, you ask? Let's see.

It's that one I would be willing to bet we've all been in a class with. The one who never seems to have to read class material, listen to the teacher, or study for a test before they come in and take it. Yet, they are the first to ace it and leave class early. There was one or more of those in a few of my classes, and I envied the results they got with what seemed to me to be little to no effort. They nonchalantly picked up their papers, which were not only marked with an "A" but also with glowing reviews handwritten off to the side by the teacher indicating how well they'd done. That student would then set that paper aside on their desk for the rest of the world to see, while they didn't even seem to take notice. They would then look around the class to see who they could talk with to pass the time. That is the student I wished I could be, even just once.

One evening, I went to collect an assignment I had turned in during one of the first classes I took at the university I attended. The teacher had bundled all the papers the class had turned in together in a box and left it in the administration's office of the college for each student to pick up on their own. I went through the papers looking for the one with my name on it. In going through them, I saw one with those words of praise written by the teacher in red. In my mind, it had to belong to that one student I described above. Imagine my surprise when I shifted my eyes to the top of that paper, looking for the name of this lucky student, and saw my own. Wow! This kind of surprise sometimes only needs to happen once to be appreciated for life.

I also overheard one of my teachers refer to me as one of his best students when speaking to another one of my classmates. Another teacher called me at home one evening, asking if I could tutor other students in her class since I happened to be doing well in it. These were the little things that gave me the confidence and the desire to keep working hard to move forward.

So, am I telling you all this to try to make myself look and feel good? Yes, and yes.

Yes, because these are some of the things I dug up from my past that helps me believe in myself and gives me more courage in fighting the battle I am up against now with my health. Since I had been strong enough and stubborn enough to hang in there for all those other things that were important to me in life at the time, I really do owe it to myself and those who love me to try to conquer the battle that is most important to us now, and that which my life depends on me winning.

And yes, again, because these are the kinds of things that I hope you look for in yourself, and when you find them, and I'm sure you will find some, I hope it helps you build the confidence you need to face and fight whatever struggles you deal with in this life. When you are brave enough to try, I will again like who I see when I look in the mirror. I will be even happier when you succeed.

We are all important, and we all have something to give. It is that gift we are born with, whether we know it or not, that waits to be opened. Often, we suppress our own success and well-being with self-doubt. There are also many poor souls, who are told so often by someone else that they will never succeed, and so, in turn, don't really try. In one of the self-help books I read (and remember, there were many of them), the author made a valid point: doubt kills many more dreams than failure does. I believe this to be true.

If we are willing to believe in ourselves and work on those attributes we are born with, they will work in our favor in this life. It makes sense that we gravitate to those things we are good at, and we normally do our best at those things we are born to do. I realize that some people are given more of an opportunity to be successful in meeting their goals than others are. Still, I believe that where there is a will, there is usually a way. Some of the most successful people in our world are those who others had little to no expectations of succeeding but who, lo and behold, ran far out in front of their competition when they tried. Success is a personal choice, not a God-given right. Though I admit, it seems so for some.

As it turns out, on this day, the 13th of December, 2022, I received a phone call from my doctor down south, informing me that there was an issue with the blood cells they collected for my upcoming therapy, and they don't recommend I use them. I sit in shock. I cannot believe what I am hearing.

This means all my upcoming appointments down south have to be canceled, as do our hotel reservations. I will now need to return to the hospital for another day of stem cell collection.

The final procedure scheduled for the 4th of January, 2023, will be postponed by a minimum of two months. You remember, the one I was putting so much faith in being that sign of hope I have been longing for.

It also means I will need to go back on the chemo infusions I thought I was done with, along with all those other meds I was taking. The thought of getting off all that shit had been beyond exciting. My excitement had spilled into the infusion room at the cancer center I go to, and the nurses who did my treatments had all been so excited for me when I told them about my upcoming therapy.

This is such a blow, and I am absolutely devastated. I gave Dave the bad news, and he, too, is devasted. Today is a hard day. Especially since just yesterday, my local oncologist would not allow me to have my regular treatments because my white blood cell counts were too low.

Did I mention I seem to have a lot of bad luck?

I pray that things will get back on track right away and therapy will follow soon after that. Somewhere there is a silver lining here, I'm sure, and I'm determined to find it. This is one of those things I ask you to do when you are dealt with yet another blow. After all, this is the underlying reason I am writing my story. However, it is also great therapy for me and gives me a greater purpose in this moment.

So, before this year, 2022 ends, I have been scheduled for another stem cell collection. It will take place on the 3rd of January. Before being admitted to the hospital, I must have a particular type of covid test and provide the results to my doctor's coordinator before we head down. This test is not available in our town, so we must go north or south to get it.

As we have plans to go south and take our son and his girlfriend to dinner, I get online and make an appointment there for my test. We drive down and pull in half an hour before the scheduled appointment time, only to be told by the young lady at the pharmacy that the store's computer system is down, and she cannot access the information on file for appointments. Therefore, she cannot test me.

Really?? Are you f**cking kidding me? I am a cancer patient scheduled to go to Los Angeles next week for a stem cell collection, which I cannot have if I cannot provide a negative result on this covid test. We just drove 50 miles to complete this test that I made an appointment online for the day before, and now you tell me your system is down, and you can't help me??

Wow! Can you say "bad luck" again?

I know this is not this young lady's fault, and there is nothing she, nor we, can do about it. We smile, say thanks, and go on our way. Because this is New Year's weekend, we are even more stressed, as Dave is convinced testing clinics will be closed for the holiday. As it turns out, I go online, and after more research and additional phone calls, I'm able to schedule the test I need for the following morning. This time, we drive north, pull up right on time for my appointment, and get it done without any problems whatsoever.

Wow, some good luck for a change. What a relief! As I said, "Where there is a will, there is usually a way!"

Since I had set a tentative goal to have this part of my story finished by the end of 2022, I will wrap up with those events that have taken place up to this point. As I now feel the same type of kinship with those of you reading these words, as I have with so many of the characters I have met throughout the years in so many of the books I have read, it is difficult now to bring my story to a close. Even if, hopefully, it is temporary.

One of my long-term goals is to sit back after we get through a successful journey with Car-T therapy and share that story with you as well. It is high on my list of reasons to keep on living, and I am so thankful this list is a long one. Remember, short- and long-term goals go there.

So, until next time, I hope to talk to you later!

Thanks for Reading *The Luck of the Draw!*
If you found my book helpful, your review can help others find my book easier. Please head over to Amazon or wherever you bought this book and leave me a review today. Your feedback matters!

Let's Connect

Thank You!

@sandrapickles60

Instagram

Sandrapickles60@gmail.com

Facebook

YouTube

Acknowledgments

First and foremost, I wish to thank my husband, Dave, for his loyal presence during this journey and for never allowing cancer to "undo" the words "I do". Secondly, I wish to thank my many family members for the steady support they have given and continue to provide for Dave and me through our trials and tribulations. You have all been and are still a true Godsend. Thank you to all my friends, neighbors, and former coworkers who cheer me on! It takes a village, and I sure do have one. I wish to give a special thanks to my wonderful friend Jennifer Fresca, who, while also suffering with cancer, keeps my spirits up with her kind words and encouragement almost daily, no matter how weary she is. It was she who referred me to the self-publishing school I joined to try to make the dream of sharing my story with the world happen. She has been a great source of encouragement to me while writing this book, as Dave cracked the whip and his brother Kevin cheered me on. A huge thanks to my editor Jeannie Culbertson for her hard work, attention to detail, and kind words of compassion as we worked side by side through our tears to piece together this part of my story.

About the Author

Sandra Pickles, whose father served in the air force, was born in Tachikawa, Japan. She enjoyed the overseas and stateside travels that being part of a military family offered. Sandra enjoys traveling, loves animals, and has a passion for reading, writing, and music. She earned an associate's degree in business management and a bachelor's degree in sociology. Sandra worked for a financial institution when her life was turned upside down after being diagnosed with cancer in October 2017. Join her on her journey in *The Luck of the Draw*, as Sandra tells her story of not only the heartbreak cancer brought into her life but also of the joys. Sandra lives in Lompoc, California with her husband, Dave, and their dog, Smokey.

Made in the USA
Las Vegas, NV
14 August 2023

76078687R00174